Susan Bulanda

Boston Terriers

Everything About Purchase, Care,
Nutrition, Breeding, Behavior, and Training

With 30 Color Photographs
Illustrations by Michele Earle-Bridges

BARRON'S

Photo Credits:
Greg and Paula Anderson: inside front cover, pages 10 (bottom, right), 27 (bottom); Susan Bulanda: page 64 (top, left); Michele Earle-Bridges: front cover, pages 9 (top and bottom, left), 10 (top), 27 (top, left), 28 (top); Verlane and Clinton House: page 63 (bottom), back cover (bottom, left); Barbara Minger: page 27 (top, right); Judith Strom: pages 9 (bottom, right), 45, 46, 63 (top), 64 (top, right); Suzanne Maxine Uzoff: pages 10 (bottom, left), inside back cover, back cover (top and bottom, right).

About the Author:
Susan Bulanda is a Pennsylvania-based dog behaviorist and trainer, who has written and lectured extensively on canine topics. She is the author of *The Canine Source Book* and *Ready: A Step-by-Step Guide for Training the Search and Rescue Dog*.

All inquiries should be addressed to:
Barron's Educational Series, Inc.
250 Wireless Boulevard
Hauppauge, New York 11788

International Standard Book No. 0-8120-1696-3

Library of Congress Catalog Card No. 93-51037

Library of Congress Cataloging-in-Publication Data

Bulanda, Susan.
    Boston terriers : everything about purchase, care, nutrition, breeding, behavior, and training / Susan Bulanda ; illustrations by Michele Earle-Bridges.
        p.   cm.
    Includes bibliographical references and index.
    ISBN 0-8120-1696-3
    1. Boston terriers.   I. Title.
SF429.B7B85   1994
636.7'2—dc20   93-51037
                                CIP

PRINTED IN HONG KONG
567 9927 98765432

Important Note:
This book is concerned with selecting, keeping, and raising Boston terriers. The publisher and the author think it is important to point out that the advice and information for Boston terrier maintenance applies to healthy, normally developed animals. Anyone who buys an adult dog or acquires one from an animal shelter must consider that the animal may have behavioral problems and may, for example, bite without any visible provocation. Such anxiety-biters are dangerous for the owners as well as the general public.

    Caution is further advised in the association of children with dogs, in meetings with other dogs, and in exercising the dog without a leash.

Contents

Contents

Preface

This is the story of one of the most "American" dogs ever bred. The Boston terrier was developed in Massachusetts by crossing dogs imported from England. The breeding was done by a group of men who felt a deep passion for tough, working dogs. After crossing English bulldogs with English terriers, the offspring were inbred for a number of generations. Fanciers of this new breed of dog were subjected to extreme prejudice and opposition in the early days, but they did not abandon their efforts.

It is interesting to note that the Boston terrier fought for its recognition in the world of the dog fanciers at the same time that the American Kennel Club was fighting to establish itself. The two grew together and gained acceptance at about the same time. One can only imagine the passionate conflicts that occurred between the different factions of the dog world over the Boston terrier.

Over the years I have known a number of Boston terriers and can recall one who lived in my neighborhood when I was growing up. He was a happy young fellow who would run to the edge of the lawn each time I went by and give me a look as if to say, "Oh, it's just you." The memory of this dog has always represented for me the essence of the Boston terrier—curious and playful, with a strong sense of self-worth.

Understanding the Boston Terrier

History of the Breed

The Boston terrier was actually developed in 1865 by a handful of coachmen living in the Beacon Hill area of Boston. They used their employers' purebred dogs as foundation stock to create a unique new breed.

The Boston terrier was developed by crossing the Old English toy bulldog with the white English terrier, and adding in a bit of French bulldog. Through inbreeding, mutations, and accidents, the Boston terrier was shaped into what it is today.

The Old English toy bulldog was similar to the Boston terrier but the breed tended to be small, and in the nineteenth century it was considered to have no useful purpose. Toy bulldogs had a following in France, and most were exported there rather than to the United States

It is said that the Boston terrier was created out of curiosity—to see what could be developed—and, perhaps, to produce a new fighting dog. But it never gained popularity as a fighter. Instead, it later became popular with women.

The early Boston terriers did not look anything like today's version, and the original Beacon Hill breeders would not at all appreciate what they would see today. Most likely, they would consider the modern breed to be much too fine and effeminate. The original Boston terrier was developed as a "man's" dog. It was not bred for markings or color but rather for its small size. This necessitated quite a bit of inbreeding.

During the nineteenth century it was common practice to prefix a dog's personal name with the last name of its owner. Thus, the ancestor of all modern Boston terriers was a dog known as Hooper's Judge. Judge lived about 1865 and was owned by a Mr. Robert C. Hooper of Boston. Mr. Hooper purchased Judge from Mr. William O'Brien, who had imported the dog from Europe.

Hooper's Judge was a cross between an English bulldog and an English terrier, with looks that favored the bulldog. The English bulldogs of that period did not resemble the breed of today, but rather the modern American Staffordshire terrier. Judge was dark brindle with a white stripe through his face and weighed about 32 pounds (14.5 kg).

According to some reports, Judge's breeder was a Mr. R. M. Higginson. His sire is said to have been a dog named Langdon's Crib, whose sire in turn was Nevin's Steel. Both Crib and Steel were said to be bulldogs. Judge was bred to a white bitch named Gyp or Kate. She weighed about 20 pounds (9 kg) and was owned by Mr. Edward Burnett of Southboro. Gyp was well built and had a three-quarter tail. Records do not show any additional matings for Hooper's Judge, so we can only wonder what became of him.

Inbreeding was subsequently carried out for a number of generations. Other imported bloodlines were then introduced into the strain. One of these was the Scottish Perry, a dog of about 6 pounds with a straight three-quarter tail. Another, the Jack Reed, was an evenly marked, rough-coated, reddish-brindle-and-white animal, weighing 12 to 14 pounds (5.4–6.4 kg), and carrying a straight three-quarter tail.

Yet another import was Kelly's Brick, a fierce dog weighing about 16 pounds (7.3 kg). He was white with black spots, had a large skull and large eyes, and, once again, a straight tail. There was also O'Brien's Ben, who was short and cobby, with a white-and-brindle coat, weighing about 20 pounds (9 kg), and also with a straight three-quarter-length tail.

The inbreeding then continued, producing Well's Eph and Tobin's Kate. From the breeding of Eph and Kate came Barnard's Tom and Atkinson's Toby. Tom and Toby were important foundations as sires for the breed. Tom had a cobby body and is credited with being the first Boston with a screw tail. This type of tail was first regarded as a deformity, but it was later established as a legitimate trait when it was traced back to a white English bulldog bitch named Fancy (whelped between 1840 and 1850). From these dogs came Summerville Countess, Princess Queen (1891), and Nancy III (1896). Tom and Toby were great dogs, and it is generally agreed that the bitches sired by them produced the most highly regarded offspring of the period.

Tom's owner, Mr. John P. Barnard, who maintained a kennel of bulldogs and bullterriers, thoroughly enjoyed his new animals. The new cross went by several names: round-headed bull and terrier, bullet head, and American bullterrier.

The first Boston terriers met with quite a bit of opposition from dog fanciers, as neither the bullterrier proponents nor the bulldog fanciers would accept the new breed. If Boston terriers were allowed at dog shows at all, they were given a separate class. In these early years the competition between the various dog clubs became nasty. At one point, the Boston-terrier fanciers launched a press campaign that attempted to portray the bulldog as a savage animal unfit for gentle society. Bulldog fanciers retaliated with claims that the Boston terrier was nothing more than a mongrel.

In 1889, after some 19 years of development, about 30 fanciers in and around Boston formed the American Bull Terrier Club and exhibited their dogs, which were called round heads or bullterriers, at local dog shows. The new club met with quite a bit of opposition from Bull Terrier Breeders, as well as from the American Kennel Club, which did not want to recognize the Boston-terrier breed.

About two years later, in 1891, the club was renamed the Boston Terrier Club of America, and the name of the breed was changed to the Boston terrier.

The bickering between the clubs continued until 1893, when the Boston terrier was officially recognized by the American Kennel Club. After that, everyone buried the hatchet, for the most part, and became friends.

By the 1920s the Boston terrier became so popular that the breed may well have accounted for 20 to 30 percent of dog-show entries of that decade.

Since that time interest has leveled off. The popularity of the Boston terrier is not limited to the United States, but has spread throughout the world, even to countries such as England, where strict quarantine requirements make it difficult to import dogs.

Some of the earliest Boston terriers to be recognized by the American Kennel Club were:

- Hector, whelped 1891, brindle and white
- Dixie, whelped 1891
- Punch, whelped 1888, fawn and white
- Mike, whelped 1893, brindle and white

The first champion of breed was a dog named Topsy, whose registration had originally been cancelled due to impure breeding.

Some of the early kennel names were: Albert Alward's Donnybrook, Edward Axtell's St. Botolphs, J.P. Barnard's Myrtle Street, F.G. Bixby's Bixbys, W.L. Davis' Willowbrook, G.B. Doyle's Doyles, A.L. Goode's Goodes, W.C. Hook's Somerville, W.G. Kendall's Squantum, F.A. Locks' Bayonne, P. McDonald's Shawmut, J. Vardum Mott's Presto, A.T. Mount's Oakmount, Myron W. Robinson's Rob Roy, G.A. Rawson's Druid, W.E. Stone's Stones, and C.F. Sullivan's Trimount.

As previously mentioned, often a dog's personal name was preceded by the owner's. Hooper's Judge, for example, indicates that the dog's name was Judge and the owner's name was Hooper. By the same token, the first part of the kennel's name frequently reflects the name of the kennel's owner—such as W.E. Stone, the owner of the kennel named "Stones." This information is important when you study pedigrees, since it helps you to identify the lines in your dog's ancestry. The study of a dog's pedigree can reveal many interesting stories about people and their dogs.

Nature of the Boston Terrier

Notwithstanding the descent of the modern Boston terrier from fighting dogs, the character of

Understanding the Boston Terrier

Showing your Boston terrier either in the breed ring or at an obedience show can be a rewarding experience for you and your pet.

the breed is such that it is often called the "American Gentleman." Although Bostons are not scrappers, true to their terrier nature, they are able to take care of themselves when threatened. They have gentle dispositions, and make excellent house dogs and companions. Boston terriers are gentle with children and very affectionate with their families. They are an intelligent breed, and are very alert. They make good watchdogs for the home, and are quick to alert the family to anything amiss.

The Boston terrier has a unique sense of humor, and generally loves to play. It would not be unusual for a Boston to size up a visitor in your home, decide that he or she is a good prospect for a game, and then run to get its favorite toy for some "throw and fetch." They are active dogs who would rather take part in family activities than be left alone.

As a Companion

Because they are affectionate and fun to have around, Boston terriers make lively, amusing companions. Since they are small, friendly dogs, people want to pet and play with them. The

Boston terrier's social nature, fun-loving spirit, and warm, soft eyes can entice people into interacting who would not play with other dogs.

But even if your dog's sole purpose in life is to keep you company, your Boston terrier should be given basic obedience training to ensure that it becomes a well-behaved dog who will be a welcome guest in any home. Any dog can be either a joy or a nuisance, depending upon how well you take care of it and how well it has learned its manners.

Sports and Activities for Your Boston Terrier

There are a number of organized activities in which you and your Boston terrier can participate, both for fun and competition.

Conformation shows: In this type of show your dog is judged against other dogs to determine which one comes closest to meeting the breed standard as set by the major registering body—the American Kennel Club.*

There are two ways to compete in conformation shows. One is to enter your dog in a "pointed" show given by the major registering bodies. Pointed shows require that you pre-enter your dog, usually a few months before the show date.

The other way is to enter your dog in a "match" show, which is not pointed. Many match shows permit pre-entry of your dog, but almost all will allow you to enter on location the morning of the show.

---

*List of dog-show organizations may be found in *The Canine Service Book* (see page 82).

During their first weeks, puppies spend most of the day sleeping and nursing. But even before their eyes are fully open, they should be cuddled gently for a moment or two at a time.

Understanding the Boston Terrier

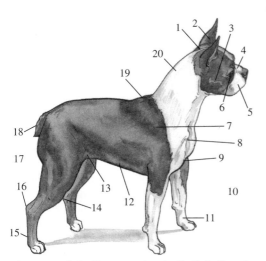

Anatomy of the Boston terrier: 1. Skull 2. Ears 3. Cheek 4. Stop 5. Eye 6. Muzzle 7. Shoulder 8. Chest 9. Brisket 10. Fore quarters 11. Front pastern 12. Rib cage 13. Loin 14. Stifle 15. Rear pastern 16. Hock 17. Hindquarters 18. Tail 19. Withers 20. Neckline

Match shows are sometimes used as testing grounds to see if a dog is good enough to be entered in a pointed show. They can provide a positive environment for the dog's owner to gain experience showing, and for the dog to get practice in the breed ring. However, for both pointed and match shows, your dog will need some training in breed-ring behavior. The handler must also learn some tricks of the trade.

The procedures for the ring are always the same. You must enter your dog in the correct class. The classes are subdivided by sex, with all dogs of the same sex competing against each other. The winner in a given class will go on to compete for "Winner's

At about four weeks of age, Boston terriers become irrepressible—joyfully exploring their surroundings and playing with anything that comes their way. (Make sure that mushrooms and other plants are nonpoisonous before allowing your puppy into an area.)

Dog" or "Winner's Bitch," which are the dogs who win over all the Boston terriers of that sex.

Next, the two winners compete for "Best of Breed." The winner of the Best of Breed competition competes for the group against all the dogs in that group. Finally, all of the group winners compete for "Best in Show."

Obedience shows: These are usually held in conjunction with conformation shows in a separate area on the show grounds. Obedience competition is open to all dogs who are registered with the sponsoring organization. The two major organizations offering obedience trials are the American Kennel Club and the United Kennel Club.

To earn an obedience degree the dog must obtain a qualifying score at three different shows under three different judges. Each qualifying score is called a "leg." Pointed shows allow you to earn legs toward an obedience title, while match shows are for practice. The titles that can be earned are:

- Companion Dog (CD)
- Companion Dog Excellent (CDX)
- Utility Dog (UD)
- Tracking Dog (TD)
- Tracking Dog Excellent (TDX)
- Obedience Title Champion (OTCH)

Boston terriers have been recognized in three different weight classes by the American Kennel Club.

Understanding the Boston Terrier

Boston terriers are generally quite capable of competing in obedience shows and earning obedience titles.

American Kennel Club Breed Standards

General appearance: The Boston terrier is a smooth-coated, short-headed, compactly built, short-tailed, well-balanced dog. It should be brindle, seal, or black in color, evenly marked with white. The head is in proportion to the size of the dog and the expression indicates a high degree of intelligence.

The body is rather short and well-knit, the limbs strong and neatly turned, and the tail is short. No feature should be so prominent that the dog appears badly proportioned. The dog conveys an impression of determination, strength, and activity with a high level of style. The carriage is

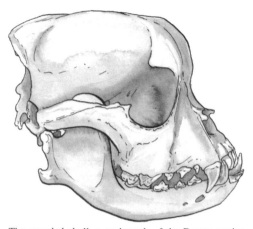

The rounded skull, a trademark of the Boston terrier, explains why the breed was once called the Round head. The Boston terrier's bite, another trademark, should be even or sufficiently undershot (the bottom extending slightly beyond the upper front teeth) to give the muzzle a square look.

easy and graceful. A proportionate combination of "color and white markings" is a distinctive feature of a representative specimen. Balance, expression, color and white markings should be given particular consideration in determining the relative value of the dog's general appearance.

Size, proportion, and substance: The weight classes of the Boston terrier are divided as follows:
- under 15 pounds
- 15 pounds to under 20 pounds
- 20 pounds to not over 25 pounds

The length of the leg must balance with the length of the body to give the Boston terrier its striking square appearance. They are sturdy dogs and must not appear either spindly or coarse. The bone and muscle must be in proportion so as to enhance the effect of the dog's weight and structure. A blocky or chunky appearance is considered a fault.

The only difference in appearance between the sexes is a slight refinement in the conformation of the bitch.

The Boston terrier's ears must be erect. They can, however, be cropped (above) or left natural (below, sometimes referred to as ("bat ears").

Understanding the Boston Terrier

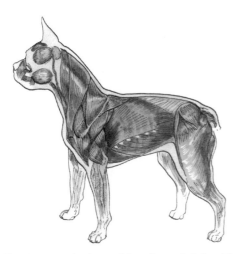

The Boston terrier is a solid, well-muscled dog. The topline slopes down at the tail.

Head: The skull is square, flat on top, and free from wrinkles. The cheeks are flat, the brow abrupt, and the stop is well defined. The eyes are wide apart, round, and large, set square in the skull, with the outside corners on a line with the cheeks as viewed from the front. They are dark in color. Any trace of blue will disqualify the animal.

Ears: The ears are small and carried erect, either naturally or cropped to conform to the shape of the head. They should be situated as near to the corners of the skull as possible.

Muzzle: The muzzle is short, square, wide, and deep in proportion to the skull. It should be shorter in length than in width or depth, and should not exceed approximately one third of the length of the skull. From the top to the end of the nose, the muzzle should be parallel with the top of the skull. It should be free of wrinkles.

The nose should be black and wide, with a well-defined line between the nostrils. A "Dudley nose," which lacks black pigmentation on all or part of the nose, will lead to disqualification.

The jaw is broad and square, with short, regular teeth. The bite is even, or sufficiently undershot to square the muzzle. The chops are of good depth, but are not pendulous. The lips should completely cover the teeth when the mouth is closed. A "wry mouth" is a serious fault.

Head faults: These include too much white, or **haw,** showing in the eyes; pinched or wide nostrils; ear size out of proportion with the rest of the head; and any showing of the tongue or teeth when the mouth is closed.

Neck, top line, and body: The length of the neck must convey an impression of balance for the total dog. It will be slightly arched, carrying the head gracefully, and be set neatly into the shoulders.

The back is just short enough to square the body. The top line is level, and the rump curves slightly to the set-on of the tail.

The chest is deep, with good width, and the ribs are well sprung, carried well back to the loins. The body should appear short.

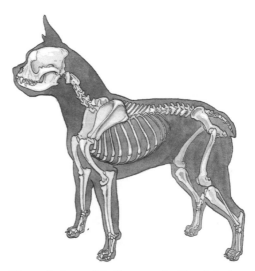

The sturdy frame of the Boston terrier. The slight slope of the rump down to the tail can be clearly seen.

The tail is short, fine, and tapering, and can be either straight or screw. It is set low and must not be carried above the horizontal line. The preferred tail does not exceed in length more than one quarter the distance from set-on to hock. A docked tail will disqualify.

Body faults: Serious body faults are a roach back, sway back, and slabsides, and a gaily carried tail.

Elbows: The elbows should be straight, without either sticking out or pointing in.

Forelegs: The forelegs are set far apart and form a nice straight line from the shoulder to the feet. The dog should not give a "bowleg" look, but should appear very strong.

Hind legs: The hind legs are bent at the stifles, short from the hocks to the feet, with the hocks set straight, turning neither in or out.

Feet: The feet are round, small, and compact, with well-arched toes.

Movement: The movement of the Boston terrier is sure-footed and straight-gaited.

Is This the Right Breed for You?

Quite frequently, someone will see a picture of a darling little Boston terrier in a magazine, dog-breed book, or on television, and fall in love with the looks of the dog. Or, having met one of these dogs, a person might be instantly captivated by its charming personality. Then, without a second thought, these people will rush out and buy one. And often they will purchase the first animal they come across.

Unhappily, after living with the dog for a while, some of these impulsive people will come to realize that Bostons have characteristics that they cannot abide. The joyous arrival of a new puppy turns into the daily nightmare of living with a dog who is not suited to the family or individual. This sad situation can be easily avoided by doing a little homework before buying a dog.

There are a number of things you can do to try to determine if a Boston terrier is the right dog for you. First, read this book. Next, contact the Boston terrier club nearest you and meet people who own the breed. You can find a club near you by contacting the American Kennel Club (see page 82) and requesting a list of the Boston terrier clubs in your state.

Once you have contacted people who actually live with a Boston terrier, you can ask them to tell you about their dog, what it is like living with one, and what they like and do not like about the breed. If possible, you should spend time visiting as many Bostons as you can. If you find one that you especially like, ask who bred the dog and contact that breeder.

There are a number of useful questions you can ask yourself to help you decide if a Boston terrier is the right breed for you:

1. What types of inherited or acquired physical problems are known to affect this breed? You must be willing to take care of any such problems that might develop in your dog. Many inherited problems can be treated or corrected, but the cost of the treatment may be more than you are willing or able to afford.

Responsible dog ownership means cleaning up after your pet. This can be easily accomplished with a pooper scooper or with a plastic bag that is inverted to cover the hand.

2. What are the grooming and general care requirements of the breed? You will need to decide whether you will groom your pet yourself or hire a groomer to take care of your dog for you.

3. How long can you expect your pet to live? Boston terriers typically have rather long life spans if well-cared for. They can live 12 years or longer.

4. Does the breed show common temperamental problems? While Boston terriers are generally sweet dogs, their temperament, which is to say their mental health, will vary from line to line and among individuals. It is important to ensure that you get a dog with a solid, sound temperament.

5. How do Boston terriers respond to training? As a rule, they are not the easiest breed to train, but with adequate knowledge, proper handling, and patience they can be taught to obey commands, and even to compete in obedience trials.

Is This the Right Breed for You?

However, you should get to know some Bostons to find out if you've got the determination and patience necessary to train one.

6. Are you (and everyone in your family) willing to care for the dog? Let's be honest about this question. Many people have neither the time nor the will to give a pet the care it needs. Children, for example, will promise the moon, only to be distracted a week later. Be sure that at least one person (you, for example) will dedicate the necessary time *every* day to adequately care for the pet. Boston terriers can become unhappy and react negatively, not to mention the possibilities of injury and disease, if they are denied attention and care.

7. Are you ready to care for a puppy or an older dog? Once again, there must be a solid commitment on the part of at least one person in your family. While puppies are engaging and cute, and for those reasons caring for them might seem relatively easy, you must bear in mind that a growing dog needs to be housetrained and learn all its manners during its first year of life. Training your dog properly will take a large bite out of your time.

Children, Other Pets, and Your Dog

When thinking about a Boston terrier, you should carefully consider any other pets you may already have in your household. If there is another dog, you must be sure that it will not harm the new one. Because they are small, one bite from a larger dog can seriously injure or even kill a Boston terrier. Similarly, your Boston terrier could be injured just by being stepped on by the larger dog. This can also be a danger if you own livestock such as horses.

Keep in mind that your Boston terrier does not think of itself as a small dog, and will not hesitate to confront larger animals.

A small puppy could easily be the victim of an intolerant or jealous cat. One swipe from a cat's claws can permanently injure your Boston terrier's eyes.

The reactions of children should be a major concern when introducing a new dog into the family. Very young children often cannot understand that the cute little doggie is not just an animated toy. Boston terriers, especially puppies, are small enough to be seriously hurt by a toddler. Also, the dog might respond by biting the child.

You must also consider elderly members of your family. As people age they may not be able to walk, hear, or see as well as before, and there is a possibility of their stumbling over or stepping on your dog. Very young puppies may not have learned to avoid the feet of family members, and will not realize that they can be hurt.

If you have any doubts as to whether a Boston terrier will work out in your household, consult a competent dog trainer, behaviorist, groomer, veterinarian, or Boston terrier breeder.

Puppy Or Older Dog

You should review the pros and cons of puppies and older dogs carefully before making your decision. Each has both positive aspects and potential negatives. Puppies will require careful training, of course. Older dogs may be well-trained or may have undesirable habits that you will have to break.

The Puppy

One of the advantages of getting a puppy is that it will grow up with you. This will give you the opportunity to socialize it to your lifestyle, and to teach it as you prefer. Your pet will grow up with a special devotion toward you and your family which it may never give to anyone else.

A puppy can be a great deal of fun, and its antics can provide you with hours of delight. On the other hand, a puppy will also need more of your time during its first year of life. It will need to be housebroken, given obedience training, taught not to chew, and so forth. And it must be carefully trained in how to interact with adults, children, and other animals. A puppy will require more veterinary care in its first year of life than the yearly maintenance it will need thereafter.

If you intend to enter your dog in conformation shows or obedience trials, a puppy will be a riskier proposition than a trained adult dog, since no one can determine in advance if it will grow up to be a good competitor.

The Older Dog

Because nowadays Boston terriers are not as popular as some other breeds, there are fewer available for adoption. However, sometimes older dogs do come up for adoption or sale. This situation can arise due to the death of the owner, or perhaps for some reason the inability of the owner to keep the dog. Sometimes a breeder will offer a retired show dog for adoption or sale. At other times the breeder may determine that a show prospect will not work out, and will put the dog out for adoption or sale.

You should also be aware that people will often put a dog up for adoption because they do not like the way it behaves. This does not necessarily mean that the dog is bad. Behavior which is not acceptable to one person may be perfectly fine, or even desirable, to another.

There are a number of points to consider when acquiring an older dog. You must be aware that the dog will need time to get used to you and your family. The adjustment period can take from three to six months. You cannot "explain" to the dog that your house is now its new home, and it cannot "tell" you about its fears and anxieties.

Sometimes a dog will appear happy and seem to fit in right away, but if you pay close attention you will see it relax and become even more playful and at ease a few months later. You will realize in retrospect that your new pet was, in reality, rather upset and on edge at first.

One of the benefits of adopting an older dog is that it will most likely be housebroken and obedience-trained. The dog will be settled and mature. It will have had all the necessary puppy shots, and will often be neutered or spayed.

If you plan to get a dog as a companion for the elderly, a mature dog may be the best choice, as such a dog will be easier for an older person to handle.

Throughout the country there are groups of people who rescue unwanted dogs of different breeds. These associations are referred to as *breed rescue groups*. A Boston terrier rescue group is a good place to find an older dog for adoption, since the people who foster the dogs will evaluate them and try to match each dog with the right home.

Male or Female

Both physically and psychologically, there is not much difference between the male and female Boston terrier. The female is generally a bit smaller than the male, but not enough to make a big difference.

The temperament in both sexes is about the same. A more important behavioral determinant is the dog's breeding. There is, however, one very important factor over which you have influence, and that is the decision whether or not to spay or neuter your pet.

Unless you are planning to make a commitment to show and breed your dog, both males and females should be "fixed." This operation will eliminate many of the problems associated with each sex. For example, an unneutered male can have accidents or "mark" in your house. This can be either an occasional problem or a regular occurrence. Male dogs can be expected to mark outside, and this can be a problem if you have gardens, unless you train your pet to relieve himself in designated areas only.

If you own an unspayed bitch she will come into "season" or "heat" twice a year. During this time you will not be able to trust her outside at all, even on a leash. Male dogs have been known to breed a bitch while she is on a leash being walked by her owner.

With an intact bitch you will risk having an unwanted litter of puppies every six months.

Both males and females who are not fixed will have a tendency to roam, the male in pursuit of a bitch, and the bitch to let the male know where she lives. Generally, the male will have a greater desire to roam than the female, and will travel a larger area. If given the opportunity, a bitch in heat will take off in search of a willing male, and you can bet that she will find one.

For small dogs, such as Boston terriers, there are added dangers inherent in unregulated breeding. If a Boston bitch breeds with a larger dog, the developing puppies may be too big for her, creating medical problems and possibly even causing the death of the dam. The actual mating itself can cause serious injury to the bitch if the male is much larger. Therefore it is especially important to spay those Boston terrier bitches that are not slated for a show or breeding program.

There are numerous medical side benefits to fixing your dog. For example, spaying your female before her first heat (between five and six months of age) will greatly reduce the risk of breast cancer. A neutered male will be calmer, making him a nicer family pet. He will be less likely to become aggressive or competitive toward other dogs, and will not chase after a bitch in heat. Neutering a male will also reduce the risk of certain types of cancer. For both sexes, the urge to roam will be reduced and, for both, the life expectancy can also be expected to increase.

What Does Quality Mean?

Whether you want a dog primarily as a pet or for show, you want to consider the various factors which, taken together, determine the "quality" of an animal. You must learn what "quality" actually means. Some of the myths and misinterpretations concerning the quality of a dog are discussed below.

Papers

It is commonly believed that if a puppy is registered, it is a quality dog. Unfortunately, this is not the case. The American Kennel Club, which is the major registering body for all dogs in this country, is simply a registry service. The registration papers which come with your dog do not guarantee anything except that a history or pedigree of a given dog has been reported to the American Kennel Club, and has been accurately recorded by that agency. Registry is not a guarantee that the puppy you purchase:

• Is healthy
• Of sound temperament
• Of show quality
• Will make a good pet
• Meets standards for the breed
• Is free of genetic defects
• Or even that the papers which accompany your puppy actually belong to that particular dog.

The validity of the papers issued with your Boston puppy as well as the quality of the puppy you purchase depend entirely upon the ethics of the breeder with whom you deal.

In some cases, a breeder will determine that a puppy has a major flaw which will bar the dog from a show career. Such puppies will be sold as pet quality (usually with a spay/neuter contract). As far as being pets, there is absolutely nothing wrong with such animals, and the overall quality of the dog will be substantially the same as the puppy's show-prospect littermates.

Where To Get a Good Boston Terrier

Once you have decided that the Boston terrier is the right breed for you, you will be faced with the problem of finding an animal of the quality you desire. This will mean locating a good, ethical breeder.

The best place to start the search for a breeder is with your national and/or local Boston terrier club, or your local Boston terrier rescue group. You can find out how to contact these organizations through the American Kennel Club.

If a local or national club meets within traveling distance of your home, attend their meetings on a regular basis. Get to know the breeders, and go see their dogs. When you find an animal you like, find out who bred the dog and contact that breeder. If the breeder does not have puppies available but seems to be someone you might trust, see if you can get on a waiting list, or ask to be referred to another breeder.

The newspaper is not the place to find good breeders. Good breeders usually have waiting lists for puppies, and do not need to advertise.

Quality Begins with the Breeder

Technically speaking, anyone who breeds dogs is considered a "breeder." This includes those people who consider their dogs "cash crops," and simply produce animals without regard for the health and welfare of the dogs. These operations, called "puppy mills," often experience a high rate of disease and mortality among their "products." In some areas of the country the puppy mill may sell directly to the public. Sometimes people find these breeders by taking a drive in the country and seeing a handmade sign in front of a quaint farmhouse offering puppies for sale. The plain clothes of the farmer and his family might make the unsuspecting buyer instantly at ease and foster a feeling of ethics and safety. However, to the puppy-mill "farmer," his puppies are just a cash crop.

Legitimate commercial breeding operations carry certain risks as well. Though the paperwork will usually be in order, the main point of these businesses is to make a profit. The operators might find themselves tempted to cut corners by minimizing medical care, socialization training, and human-animal bonding activities. There will also be more of a chance for a substandard animal to be released from such an operation, as every dog not sold is a financial loss. Puppies produced by puppy mills and commercial breeders are hardly ever of show quality, and many do not even make good pets.

Good breeders and serious hobbyists will want to sell their puppies themselves so they can personally evaluate the prospective buyer. They will offer a health guarantee and will take the puppy back if there is a problem. Ethical breeders put their hearts and souls, as well as a great deal of work, into producing a good line of dogs. They will know each animal personally, and will want to place their puppies in a good home.

A good breeder will maintain certain policies as a matter of course. You should ask specifically about the following matters:

1. Will the breeder stand behind the dog for its entire life?

This does not mean that if your dog catches a communicable disease, or is killed in an accident, or dies of old age, that you will get the dog replaced. But it does mean that if your dog develops any inherited or congenital diseases or physical flaws, the breeder will replace the dog or at least work with you to take care of the problem. A good breeder wants to know how his or her dogs develop throughout their lives, as this is the only way to develop good, strong lines.

2. Will the breeder help you with any questions you may have concerning all aspects of dog ownership?

Where To Get a Good Boston Terrier

Good breeders want you to be happy with your dog. They do not want you to have to return the dog to them, because this is not in the best interests of the animal. Therefore, they will help you in any way they can, and will try to answer questions you may have about your dog.

3. Will the breeder tell you about faults of the line and the breeding?

There are no perfect dogs. A concerned breeder will tell you as soon as any problem develops in the line, so that you can look for the problem in your pet. You should be warned about any possible defects which might show up in your Boston terrier.

4. Will the breeder give as references people who have purchased their dogs?

Honest breeders are proud of what they have produced, and will welcome any opportunity to show off. They will be delighted to know that you want to see their stock and find out how their dogs turn out. It goes without saying that they will want you to talk to satisfied customers.

5. Does the breeder give the bitch and puppies the best food, veterinary care, and socialization?.

A concerned breeder will provide the best care for both the puppies and the dam. This will ensure that you will own a happy, healthy dog.

6. Will the breeder require you to sign a contract stating that you will adhere to the breeder's or breed club's breeding ethics?

Concerned breeders want to ensure that their dogs will be given the best of care, and that you will observe the highest ethical standards with your dog. A contract keeps everything clear, and protects both the seller and buyer.

On the other hand, there are certain warning signs of a bad breeder. Watch out for the following:

1. Breeders who do not offer to guarantee the puppy for life against genetic defects. A good breeder will want to know why a dog dies, and will want to determine whether the dog has a genetic defect or not.

2. Breeders who offer a blanket replacement guarantee. You must be careful about this. Some breeders mass-produce so many puppies that they can offer to replace any dog, regardless of why it dies. A mass-production breeder is, by definition, paying less attention to each animal.

3. Breeders who produce many litters per year. The American Kennel Club considers someone who breeds more than ten litters in a year to be worth investigation as a puppy mill. The United Kennel Club feels that anyone who breeds more than six litters per year should be investigated. It is very difficult to monitor and follow up on a great many puppies at the same time. You should, therefore, seriously question the breeder as to the number of litters being produced each year.

4. Breeders who produce more than one litter at a time. Again, it is very difficult to give each puppy the care and attention it requires during the critical first seven weeks of life. The difficulty is compounded when there are two different litters, especially if they are of different ages.

5. Breeders who produce more than one or two breeds of dog. Yet again, there is the matter of volume. It is possible to keep up on the latest medical and genetic developments and to keep accurate records on more than one breed, but the difficulty of the task increases with the number of animals involved. It is very hard to work or show numerous dogs from different breeds.

This does not mean that a breeder should not own different breeds, but to do a quality job of breeding more than two breeds at the same time is a monumental task. Puppy mills will usually mass-produce many different breeds of dog.

6. Breeders who do not maintain clean facilities. This is a sign of someone who is trying to cut corners or has become overextended. You can tell the difference between the breeder whose litter has just messed up the puppy pen from one who does not clean on a daily basis.

Where To Get a Good Boston Terrier

7. Breeders who keep their dogs outside all the time. Even in milder climates, Boston terriers should not be kept as outdoor dogs. A breeder who is maintaining this arrangement is not working for the best interests of the breed and should be avoided.

8. Breeders who do not have a good socialization program. All puppies need to be handled and given a certain amount of socialization during the first seven weeks of their lives. An unsocialized dog will have behavior problems, which will lower its quality. A concerned breeder will have developed a program to ensure that only the best-quality dogs are sold. Those who do not have such a program, or who have no idea what a socialization program is, should be avoided.

9. Breeders who do not question you carefully to find out if the Boston terrier is the best breed for you. A breeder who has put heart, soul, and money into producing a top-quality dog will want to know as much about you as possible to determine that you will make a good owner. Not everyone will be happy with a Boston terrier. A breeder who does not question you is either a novice or does not care.

10. Breeders who do not require a breeding contract. A concerned breeder will ask you to sign a contract which will include terms that are in the best interests of the dog you purchase. The contract will include some "if/then" clauses which will determine what will happen in certain specific circumstances. For example, the dog may develop an inherited defect, or become ill, or you may become unable to keep the dog any longer, and so forth. If you are not offered a contract it may be because the breeder is not interested in the dog after it leaves the kennel.

11. Breeders who push for "breeder's terms." This phrase usually means that you will be required to breed your dog and return many or all of the puppies to the breeder. Any breeder who wants a litter or two as part payment for the dog you are getting is someone who is mainly concerned with making a profit. A breeder who requires you to sign a contract when your puppy is still young saying that you will breed the dog once or twice, is obviously a breeder who is not concerned with whether or not the puppy will grow up to be breeding quality but someone who just wants some extra puppies to sell.

12. Breeders who have never bred a litter before. A novice breeder should be working with a qualified, experienced, reputable breeder who can help him or her out. You will want to know who the mentor is, and talk with that person if possible. If the novice is going it alone, you should be very careful to check with the breeder of his dogs. While everyone must start somewhere, it is usually best to go with those who work with the blessings of their peers.

Remember, geographical location, ethnic background, or religious affiliation of the breeder do not affect the quality of your Boston terrier. The only guarantee of quality is the personal ethics of your breeder.

Playing with mom and with each other is an important part of a young Boston terrier's socialization.

Where To Get a Good Boston Terrier

How To Select the Right Boston Terrier

Once you have located a reputable breeder, the next decision you will be faced with will be which puppy from which litter? Here are some questions you can ask to help you make your choice.

Question the breeder about the parents of the litter. Ideally you will want to see both the sire (male) and the dam (female). If they are not available, you should at least try to see photos of each. You will need to know that the parents of the litter are healthy, friendly, and conform to the breed standard. You will want to see the pedigree papers.

Ask the breeder to give you as much information about the line and the dog as possible. A good breeder will have many stories to tell about the dogs in the pedigree.

Temperament (the dog's mental health) and obedience titles will be more important to you than the number of champions in the pedigree. Championship only indicates that a dog's conformation (how it looks and moves) measures up to

The Boston terrier family. If possible, try to see both the mother and the father of your prospective pup.

the breed standard. It gives no indication of temperament or intelligence, which are the qualities that make a good pet.

Just as you will want to question the breeder about the operation, the breeder will want to ask you many questions about your lifestyle and how you plan to take care of your new Boston terrier. Expect to be questioned closely concerning your home environment and work schedule, your plans for your dog, your ideas regarding training, your veterinarian, and so on. This is how the breeder will form an idea of which puppy will suit your personality, lifestyle, and home environment, so the puppy will have the best chance for a happy life.

It will be a big help if your breeder is experienced enough to select a puppy for you. The breeder will be a much better judge of each dog's temperament, because each has been observed from birth.

You can also ask the breeder to have the puppies temperament tested for temperament with a **Puppy Aptitude Test (PAT).** If this has not been done, ask if you may hire a competent trainer to do it for you.

If you cannot find a qualified trainer, use this general rule of thumb: For an average pet, do not take the boldest puppy in the litter, the one who runs to you first and pushes the other puppies out of the way. Such an animal may be difficult to handle. Many people feel that the boldest puppy instantly fell in love with them and fought to be the first to reach them, but this is not the case. The dog just wanted to maintain its position as a bully, and may try to push you around as well.

You do not want the smallest puppy either. This could be an indication of medical or developmental problems that would not show up until later.

You probably will not want a puppy who is shy and timid either. Such an animal may have difficulty facing the challenges of life, and may not make a well-adjusted pet.

After eliminating the extremes, choose a puppy who seems interested in you and wants to spend a lot of time with you, the one who is most willing to follow you around. This kind of behavior indicates good balance in mind and body, with a desire to be near humans.

Often a litter consists of only one or two puppies, and they are so close in all aspects that the choice comes down to the one whose looks appeal to you most. And that can be all right, too.

All of the puppies in the litter should be healthy. Their coats should have a healthy shine and they should be neither too fat nor too thin. You should be able to just feel the ribs when you run your fingers over their sides. They should not have fleas and should be clean, with no strong, offensive odor. Watch for disease symptoms such as runny eyes, discharge from the nose, bald patches, sores, etc.

What Age To Get a Puppy

Many behaviorists feel that you should get your new puppy at the beginning of the seventh week. However, if you have small children, other pets, or circumstances which would not be advantageous for a younger animal, you may want to leave the puppy with the breeder until it is 12 weeks old. A good breeder will provide the puppy with the important socialization and training needed between 7 and 12 weeks.

You should never take a puppy from its mother before seven weeks, since the puppy needs interaction with its mother and littermates until that age. Breeders who are anxious to save money will let puppies go at five and six weeks of age. You do not want to get a puppy from that type of operation.

When To Get a Boston Puppy

Although almost any time can be a good time to get your new puppy, a little planning can be advantageous. If you work and have vacation time, it is best to plan a few days off to stay home with your new puppy. This will give your new pet time to bond with you, and it will feel more secure after a few days with you than if it is brought to a new home and left completely alone the very next day. If you cannot take off a day or two, try to bring your puppy home on the evening before you have a few days off, such as a Friday night. This will allow the puppy time to get adjusted. You will be able to take it to the veterinarian for a check-up, and you will be there if the puppy has trouble getting used to different water, food, surroundings, climate, etc. This last is very important for puppies who are shipped from other parts of the country.

Some people feel that it is easier to housetrain a Boston terrier in the spring because they do not like to take the puppy outside when it is cold.

The arrival of the new puppy should be during a quiet time in your life. Being taken to a new home can be very stressful; you cannot "explain" the new situation to the puppy. Nor can you tell it that you want very much to make the transition as easy and nonthreatening as possible. There are certain times when it is not wise to bring a puppy home, such as holidays, birthdays, or any other time when exciting or traumatic events are taking place. The puppy will be aware of the excitement and tension felt by the family members, and this could add to the stress of being removed from the litter. Your new pet deserves a nice, quiet, loving welcome to his new home.

Caring For Your Boston Terrier

Preparing for the Arrival of Your Boston Puppy

There are some things you will need to do before you bring your new puppy home. A special place must be prepared for your pet and the rest of the house made either off limits or puppy-proofed. You will need to establish rules and procedures for the care of the puppy, and these rules must be discussed and agreed to by all of the members of your household. And there are a number of supplies you will need to have on hand.

A Place of Its Own

Dogs are territorial animals, and your puppy will need a place it can think of as its own. You should provide a quiet spot where your puppy can be alone if it wants to. This can be a corner of a room. The spot should contain your pet's sleeping area. You may want to use a child's playpen to keep your new puppy in while you are not at home. This is an ideal, safe way to keep a puppy out of trouble and still allow it enough room to exercise. You can spread newspapers on the bottom of the playpen to take care of accidents.

A crate is an ideal, safe place for a puppy. But make sure that ventilation is adequate. In general, the more open work in the structure, the better it will be for your pet.

If you do not plan to keep your puppy in a playpen, you should puppy-proof the areas where it will be allowed to go. Puppy-proofing is very similar to child-proofing. Remove from reach any objects that you do not want chewed. This includes all electrical wires and appliances. It would not hurt to put protective covers on those outlets that are at puppy level. Be sure that floor tiles, woodwork, and other surfaces are not painted or treated with toxic materials that would harm your puppy if accidently chewed or licked. It does not take a large quantity of a toxic substance to kill a small Boston terrier puppy. Be sure all cabinets are safe from prying puppy paws. This is especially necessary if you plan to confine your pet to the kitchen or bathroom. Cleansers are a major risk. Be sure to keep a poison hot-line number by your telephone in the event of an accident. The University of Illinois Veterinary Medicine Animal Poison Control Center phone number is 1-800-548-2423. You will be charged for the consultation. There are also local poison-control centers. Consult your veterinarian.

Be sure to close off any areas that you do not want the puppy to get into, such as porches, decks, balconies, or fences. You must be concerned about your pet slipping through fences, gates, or iron grillwork. If you have a fenced-in yard, be sure that there are no little holes for the puppy to squeeze through the minute your back is turned. Even if there is only one small hole in your fence, your puppy will find it! You must also be careful around stairs. A clumsy little puppy can easily slip on stairs. A puppy falling down a long flight of stairs could be seriously hurt or even killed. The most dangerous steps are the type which have open risers.

You must go over all of the dangers in your house with all of the members of your family. Everyone must learn to watch out for the puppy, so as not to step on it or catch it in a closing door. Because Boston terriers are very intelligent dogs, it should not take long before the puppy learns to avoid some of the dangers of your home. But until that time you must watch out for it.

Supplies

Basic supplies include food and water, bowls to put them in, a bed, toys, a leash and collar, and grooming equipment. It is a good idea to find out which food the breeder uses and buy that brand. This will provide some continuity in your pet's life, so that it will have something familiar in the midst of all the new experiences. Make sure that food and water bowls are as tip-proof as possible. It is better to have two separate bowls rather than two bowls in one container. If the bowls are attached you will have to disturb both water and food each time you want to change one.

You should provide a special sleeping area for your pet. This can be a basket with a blanket in it, but a canine carrying crate has a number of advantages which should be considered. It will provide the puppy with a secure feeling, and facilitate housetraining. While it is not a good idea to keep a dog crated all day long, having it sleep in a crate will help it to get used to being in one in the event that you need to transport your pet. Many people use plastic crates with small openings on the sides and wire door in the front. This may be satisfactory for many breeds of dogs, but if you plan to use it in the summer you may want to purchase an open wire-type crate instead. This will allow better air circulation in the summer, when hot weather can make it difficult for a Boston terrier to breathe. You can purchase a crate cover for an open wire crate for use in cooler temperatures or when you want to keep your pet warm. The crate should be large enough to hold a full-grown Boston terrier with a few inches to spare. An adult dog should be able to stand up and turn around. You will need to supply soft bedding which can be easily changed or cleaned. This can be anything from an old towel to special, washable imitation lambswool.

You must provide your pet with some toys to chew on. Ideally these will be tough, synthetic "bone" products or a small "Tuffy/Kong" toy, into which you can occasionally insert tiny treats. The puppy should not have rawhide, real bones, or soft plastic toys which can be chewed into little pieces and swallowed. It is not a good idea to give it old shoes, slippers, or any other type of clothing. Puppies cannot tell the difference between old shoes and new, and may chew up the new pair of shoes you were going to wear to the party tomorrow night.

You will need a collar and leash. Make sure the leash is strong without being too heavy. Never put a choke-type collar on a puppy. A very safe brand is the Premier collar. Be sure to obtain the proper kind of brush for your dog. Because their coat is short, Boston terriers need a soft bristle brush. Wire brushes can hurt their skin. A special flea comb is also necessary to check your dog for fleas.

You will also want to have nail clippers on hand, as well as some styptic powder to stop the bleeding if you should happen to clip the nails too short. (Do your best to avoid the pink "quick," but mishaps may occur from time to time.) Kwik-Stop is one brand available for this purpose.

Bringing Your New Puppy Home

When the day finally comes to take your darling little puppy home you will be very excited, but you should attempt to remain calm. If you are going to drive to pick up your pet, it will be best to transport it home in its new crate. As tempting as it may be to let the puppy sit on your lap, this is not a safe way to travel. It is best to keep the new puppy in its new crate, which you have lined with newspapers and an old towel. This way, you will keep it from wiggling off your lap and onto the floor, where it could easily crawl under a seat and get into trouble. If the puppy has a nature call or gets sick in your lap or on the floor of the car, it can be very distracting.

Be sure to bring along plenty of paper towels and water in a container just in case. If children are along for the ride, do not allow them to poke at the puppy, play with it, or jostle its crate. Try to make the ride as quiet as possible to reduce stress. If you want to play music on the radio, select something peaceful and soothing.

If the trip is going to be long, be sure to stop often to allow the puppy to exercise and take nature breaks. Be sure to keep your new pet on a leash when you do this so that it cannot run away or get hurt. Do not feed the puppy during the trip unless you plan to be driving more than six hours. You can give it a few laps of water, but do not let

When picking up and holding the Boston terrier puppy, always support both the front and the rear.

it drink too much or it may get sick. If the puppy sleeps during the trip be sure to take it out as soon as possible after it wakes up, as it will surely need a nature break.

When You First Arrive Home

When you arrive home be sure to give the puppy a chance to walk outside and take a break before going inside. As soon as your bring your pet inside, take it to the special place you have prepared, and let it explore and settle down. If your trip lasted more than four hours you can give the puppy a small amount of food and water right away, otherwise it is best to wait a little while for things to calm down.

After about an hour, you can give the puppy something to eat (if it is his normal feeding time) and drink. After eating and drinking the puppy may want to sleep. If this is the case be sure to take it out as soon as it wakes up.

Generally, you should let the puppy decide what it wants to do rather than forcing it to do what you want. Only play with it if it wants to. Let it sleep when it is tired. Try to give it at least a day to settle in before allowing friends to come and meet your delightful new friend. It would also help to keep the household quiet for at least the first day until the puppy has had a chance to explore and feel secure about its new home.

How To Carry Your New Puppy

You should never hold a puppy under its front legs with the hind legs hanging down for an

Properly socialized Bostons adore children and adults. They will even tolerate a costume contest (bottom) so long as their own special people are near by.

extended period of time. Nor should you pick up your puppy by the scruff of the neck as the mother dog does.

It is very important to teach children how to hold a puppy properly since they have a tendency to hold them under their front legs and swing them around. Puppies should be carried in such a way that the entire body is supported. Always maintain a firm grip on the puppy so that it cannot wriggle out of your hands and fall. For a small Boston puppy, a fall from three to four feet up can cause serious injury.

There are two ways to carry a puppy safely. One is to hold it with one hand supporting its front and the other hand supporting its back. With a puppy who rests quietly while being held, your can lay its entire body along your arm with the legs hanging down on either side.

Socialization

If you get a seven-to-eight-week-old Boston terrier puppy you should allow it a few days to get used to you, your family, and your home. After this time, and provided your pet has been to the veterinarian for a check-up and shots, you can start a socialization program.

Socializing a puppy is one of the most important things you can do to ensure that it grows up to be a happy, well-adjusted dog. An unsocialized puppy can grow up to become so fearful and destructive that it will have to be destroyed. A well-socialized puppy is a happy puppy, and will grow up to be a happy adult dog who will be able to take things as they come.

Bostons get along well with large dogs (top)—perhaps because they regard themselves as big dogs in small bodies. They also make good buddies for other Bostons (bottom).

Puppies do not have the life experience needed to handle many of the strange sounds, sights, and smells that they will encounter. It is easy to forget that the new puppy has only been alive for seven or eight weeks, and that it was isolated with its mother for the first five of them. Also, keep in mind that in one year your puppy is going through all of the mental and physical growth stages that humans take decades to accomplish. You do not have years to accomplish a meaningful socialization process, but months at best.

An important part of the socialization program must include handling your puppy. If your breeder has done a good job, you can continue the training where it was left off. You must touch all parts of your dog's body. This will get your dog used to being handled, and in time it will come to enjoy the contact. It will also make for a much easier job if you or your veterinarian need to give medical attention to your pet. Grooming will be easier as well.

You will want to handle the dog's face, ears, mouth, belly, feet, tail, toes, toenails, and the pads of its feet. Be sure to reward your pet for letting you do these things to it. Get your puppy used to

Always supervise the interaction between dogs and children.

being rolled over onto its back, held down on its side, and being held in your arms.

The next part of socialization occurs outside the house. You should begin by taking your new puppy to many different places, such as the park, for a walk down the street, to a playground, to watch children play, to puppy kindergarten classes, to friends' houses, etc. In other words, any place that is safe, yet active.

You do not want to subject your puppy to loud noise at close range or to other situations that may frighten it. Use your judgement as to what is safe. Also, bear in mind that some puppies seem to go through a "fright" stage at around eight weeks of age. If you notice that your pet seems unusually unsure or cautious, try to be more protective until this phase has passed.

Because Boston terrier puppies are so cute and small, you may experience a tendency to want to carry it around. This is not a good practice, because the puppy may become dependent upon you and become frightened when you put it down. It is important to avoid cuddling the puppy too much, or becoming overprotective. This, too, could develop into overdependency. If this happens you will find it difficult to leave your pet alone without its suffering anxiety.

If the puppy develops into an anxious dog, it may become destructive, or a nonstop barker. It is best to try to solve these problems when the dog is young.

A well-socialized puppy will make a good companion who will enjoy going places with you and having fun, and who will be capable of being left alone when necessary without becoming sad.

As soon as the puppy is old enough, you should start obedience training. Most trainers will not start a dog on obedience training until it is six months of age. If you cannot find a trainer who will start your dog at a younger age, you must enroll the dog in a puppy kindergarten class. Using gentle and informal methods, puppies can be taught obedience from eight weeks of age.

Some people feel that their dogs listen to them well enough without training, but even a well-behaved dog should receive obedience training. A well-behaved dog is always a welcomed guest. An obedience-training class is also part of your dog's socialization. (See page 67 for a discussion of obedience training.)

As your Boston terrier gets older, you should continue to take it to as many places as possible so that your pet does not become a "house potato."

Boarding Your Boston Terrier

If you find it necessary to board your pet, be sure that the dog has had all of its shots. You should check with your veterinarian to determine what your dog needs. Your will want to ask for referrals as to which boarding kennel to use. Consult a number of professionals, such as your veterinarian, dog groomer, pet-supply store, and dog trainer. Once you have a number of possible kennels to choose from, go and see the facilities.

The boarded dogs should look reasonably happy and clean. There should not be a strong, offensive odor. The dogs should have adequate space to exercise, and there should be an organized exercise program for them. Cats, dogs, and birds should not be kept in the same room. The kennel should have a flea-control program, and you should ask the manager to explain it to you in detail.

With a little bit of research, you should be able to find a place where you can leave your dog without worry or concern. Most dogs find the activities at a boarding kennel interesting, and do not pine for their owners. In many cases, dogs who are left at a boarding facility have a good time.

Be sure to let your veterinarian know that your dog is being boarded, and leave instructions as to how you want your dog cared for in the event of an emergency. You must also give the kennel manager instructions to contact your veterinarian.

Caring For Your Boston Terrier

You can bring along your dog's favorite toy or blanket if you wish, but often these items will get lost in the shuffle of the day-to-day kennel operation. So do not send along your best toys or blankets. An old towel will give your dog something that has your scent on it to snuggle into. You should also bring along your dog's food. Boarding kennels vary as to what they feed their boarders; often they will use one brand of food for all of the dogs. Even if this is a premium-quality food, it may upset your dog's digestion just because it is different, and cause your dog to develop diarrhea. Also remember to bring any medication your dog needs while you are away, with detailed written instructions for use. If your dog is due to get heartworm medication be sure to include it. If you are worried that your dog will not accept being boarded at a kennel, you can ease the dog into the situation with a little bit of planning.

After you select which kennel to use, make arrangements to visit with your dog. Ask one of the kennel attendants to play with your pet while you are there. Repeat the visits a few times over a couple of weeks. Next, leave your dog at the kennel for a few hours while you are at home. Repeat this, leaving your dog at the kennel a couple times a week for a few weeks. Once your dog is accustomed to this arrangement, you can leave your dog at the kennel overnight. If your dog can handle an overnight stay it should be all right for the duration of your vacation. More importantly, you will enjoy your vacation more knowing that your dog is happy and safe. Nothing spoils a vacation more than worrying about your dog.

Even if you regularly take your dog on vacation with you, it is a good idea to have a kennel you and your dog feel comfortable with. This way, in the event of an emergency, you will have a place you can use at a time when added stress would be unwanted.

There are some alternatives to boarding your pet if you must leave it at home when you travel. One possibility is to have a pet sitter take care of your dog. Pet sitters are people who will come to your home a number of times a day to walk, feed, and play with your dog while you are away. You should always interview a pet sitter and ask for references. Once you select someone, ask him or her to come over while you are home to learn the routines and know where everything is kept. This will also allow the dog and the pet sitter to get to know each other. Sometimes a neighbor can watch your dog while you are gone and act as a pet sitter. Sometimes a pet sitter may stay in your home and be a house sitter as well. This will help to ensure that your home and dog are safe while you are away. Always be sure to leave detailed instructions for the sitter, explaining what needs to be done. Go over these instructions with the sitter to make sure that they are understood.

Another alternative to a boarding kennel is to allow your dog to stay with friends or relatives. Again, a preintroduction to the friend or relative would make the stay for your dog much less stressful, and detailed, written instructions should be left with the dog.

Traveling By Car with Your Boston Terrier

If you wish to take your dog traveling with you, even if it is only down the street to a store, you must take some precautions. First, you must be sure that your pet is secure in your vehicle. You do not want to risk opening a car door and having the dog bolt out and run away. You can either crate your dog when you travel or you can purchase a harness and car-safety strap that attaches to your seat belt. It is not a good idea to tie the dog by a neck collar, because sudden stops can injure its neck and spine.

You should never leave your dog unattended in a vehicle. Boston terriers are small dogs and easier to steal than larger dogs. And in the summer you must be careful about the temperature in the car. It can quickly get very hot inside a closed vehicle. Because Boston terriers have a brachycephalic skull with a "pushed-in nose," they are prone to heat stroke and may have difficulty breathing in hot conditions. If you must leave your dog in the car, you will have to leave the windows partially open, but this might allow the dog to jump out or might allow someone to steal it.

When traveling with your Boston in the summer, you must put the air conditioning on for the dog. If you do not have air conditioning you should leave the windows open enough to allow air to circulate in the car. All dogs like to hang out of car windows, but this is a very bad idea and very dangerous for the dog. A small dog like a Boston terrier could easily fall out of a moving car. It could also be struck by flying objects, which could permanently damage the dog's eyes or even cause blindness. Never allow the dog to hang out of the windows of a moving car.

Be sure to always carry plenty of water for the dog to drink and to douse it with if it is hot and heat exhaustion is possible. In the winter, you may want to provide a sweater to keep your pet warm.

When taking long trips, be sure to allow your dog to have rest stops every two to three hours. Always use a leash with even the most well-behaved dog, both to prevent theft and to keep it from running away. Some sort of permanent identification such as a tattoo or an implanted microchip will help if your dog is lost. Carry a recent photo of your dog and be sure that your dog has visible tags on its collar, such as its license, and rabies and identification tags. Also be sure that you have all of your up-to-date shot records with you as well. This will help in the event of an emergency.

Some Boston terriers may experience motion sickness. Always limit the amount of water and food you allow your dog to have before going for a ride, even if it is a short "getting-used-to-the-car" trip. If a longer excursion is planned, you should withhold food for approximately four to six hours, and water for some two hours prior to departure. You can try to prevent motion sickness by getting your pet used to traveling in the car. This is best done by taking the puppy for short rides to fun spots, such as parks or friends' houses. Do not limit the dog's car rides to trips to the veterinarian or the puppy will develop negative associations about the car. By gradually increasing the length of the car trip, your Boston terrier will look forward to going for rides in the car. For those dogs who still experience motion sickness, you should consult with your veterinarian to determine if medication is appropriate. With a little bit of planning on your part, you can travel with your Boston terrier and both of you can have a fun, safe trip.

Traveling by Air with Your Boston Terrier

If you must transport your pet with you by air, you should check with the airline well in advance. Each airline has its own procedures for handling animals, and there are a number of federal and local statutes which may apply. Some airlines allow dogs in crates to travel with you in the passenger section of the airplane if the crate will fit under the seat. Others require that it be shipped in the cargo area, and some airlines do not allow dogs at all.

If you must ship your dog and cannot carry it onto the plane with you, be sure to research the trip carefully. Be sure to get the names of anyone you speak to so that you can follow up in the event of a problem. Dogs can be shipped in a number of ways: air freight, counter to counter, excess baggage, and in the cabin. Some airlines have limits as to how many dogs are allowed on an airplane and it is possible, should enough people show up with dogs, that you could be rerouted because of your pet.

When shipping your Boston terrier, your primary concern should be the dog's ability to breathe and to keep cool or warm. This is especially important if the dog is to be shipped in the cargo area of the airplane. Remember, a Boston terrier does not have the thick fur needed to withstand very cold temperatures, nor the ability to breathe well in very hot conditions. Be sure to discuss the trip with your veterinarian to determine the need for airsickness medication or tranquilizers.

Your crate will need to meet the airline's regulations and should be clearly marked with stickers that indicate that there is a live animal within, as well as your name, address, and phone number. You should also include a phone number where you can be reached at your destination as well as your home number.

If you can drive to a main airport, you may avoid changing flights which always presents an extra risk of losing your dog. A direct flight is always the best way to go when traveling by air.

You will want to arrive very early at the airport to allow your dog one last chance to walk and take a nature break. Before it is loaded on the airplane you will want to check the dog's crate to ensure that there are no loose nuts and bolts, or other problems. Always check the crate door to be sure that it is fastened properly. Be sure that the airline conversion kit, which allows the dog to be watered from outside the crate, is in place. Take enough food for your dog, as well as any medication it may need until you arrive home. This is especially important if you are going on vacation and will not be home for a week or so.

Keep in mind that how your dog is treated, how it is shipped, and what you are allowed to do depends upon the regulations and personnel of the airline. Do not be afraid to talk to people and insist on the type of care you want your dog to have. Be polite, but firm. Your pet's comfort and safety depends on you.

The Animal Welfare Act, which was amended in 1985, protects animals who are transported by air. For a copy of this law, contact the United States Department of Agriculture (USDA). Your local library should be able to provide you with more information about the USDA. Also, see page 82 for useful references and addresses.

Feeding Your Boston Terrier

Diet is Important

We have all heard the expression "You are what you eat." Although usually applied to humans, this nutritional cliche is equally true for dogs. If you want your puppy to grow up to be the best possible dog, you must feed it the best possible food. Young dogs often look healthy no matter what they eat, but as they get older they will show the effects of a poor diet.

Nutritious food gives your Boston terrier the ability to withstand illness, the stress of routine health care (such as dental work, spaying, or neutering), and the minor scrapes and bruises which are an inevitable result of an active dog's life. A good diet will help your dog to live longer and to remain healthier.

What is a good diet? It is one that is nutritionally complete and includes plenty of fresh, clean water. Water is often an overlooked part of a dog's diet. It must be fresh, which means you must change it a few times a day. This is very important all year round. People often forget to keep their dog's water fresh in winter because the dog does not seem to drink as much.

A mat under the food and water dishes will make it easier to keep the area clean.

Types of Dog Food

Many new types and varieties of dog food come on the market each year. As they do, it becomes increasingly difficult to determine which food is best for your dog. Because many manufacturers claim that their product is the best value, and all claim to meet canine needs, it will be up to you to determine which food is really best for your pet.

Dog food falls into three basic categories:
• dry
• wet
• semi-moist

Protein and fat content are generally offered in the following combinations:
• high protein–high fat
• medium protein–medium fat
• high protein–medium fat
• low protein–low fat

The quality of the ingredients generally ranges from "super premium" through "premium," "performance," "regular," to "economy."

Although virtually all commercial dog foods will provide adequate nutrition for your dog, some will be superior and others may not work as well. The prime determinant will be your dog. You will want to choose a food that keeps your pet active and good-looking, one that will not cause it to become either overweight or underweight.

The Basics of Nutrition

To make intelligent decisions about the different kinds of dog food, you must first understand the basics of nutrition. It is not sufficient simply to know that proteins, carbohydrates, and fats, along with vitamins and minerals, are needed for good health. You must also understand the role of each nutrient and how they work together.

Fats: In a well-balanced diet the dog gets energy from carbohydrates, proteins, and fats. However, a concentrated source of energy for dogs is fat. Generally, poultry fat is recommended, because it is less saturated and more easily digested than tallow (fat from mammals: beef, horse, pork, etc.) Fats, which provide almost twice the usable energy (measured in calories) as the same amount of carbohydrates, make food taste better to your dog. Fats also help the fat-soluble vitamins—A, D, E, and K—become available for utilization in your dog's system. Fats also provide your Boston terrier with essential fatty acids, which are required to regulate your dog's metabolism and develop healthy cells.

Be aware that the terms *fats* and *oils* are often used interchangeably; however there are differences. Fats tend to be solid at room temperature while oils are liquid. Fats are usually of animal origin while oils generally come from plants.

Protein: Protein along with fat and carbohydrates supply the dog with energy. When there are enough carbohydrates and fat to meet the dogs energy needs, protein is used to build and maintain the dog's body. Because it plays a vital role in developing healthy, strong bones, teeth, nerves, and muscles, protein is critically important in the growth of young puppies. Protein is also vital for the repair of any damage sustained by the body and for the production of antibodies.

Protein can come from both plant and animal sources, including meat, milk, cheese, eggs, and fish, as well as wheat germ, brewer's yeast, and soybean meal. In plants, it is the seeds and growing leaves which bear a significant quantity of protein, while in animals it is generally high in all tissues. However, some parts of the animal are more digestible than others. For example, both meat and bone have protein, but meat is digested more completely than bone; therefore, the dog absorbs more protein from meat.

Carbohydrates: Carbohydrates, which come mainly from plants, include both sugars and starches and can vary greatly in digestibility. As with fats and proteins, the more digestible a given carbohydrate, the more useful it will be for your dog.

Less digestible carbohydrates, usually referred to as *fiber,* are necessary to keep the digestive system working at optimum levels and preventing diarrhea or constipation. A common fiber found in dog food is beet pulp. The more digestible carbohydrates include meals ground from corn, wheat, oats, and rice.

Vitamins and minerals: These are just as important to your dog's diet as protein, fat, and carbohydrates, but the quantities required are comparatively small. Vitamins are needed to maintain good health in dogs of all ages, and to sustain growth in young dogs. With the exception of vitamin C, dogs cannot produce their own vitamins; consequently, they are dependent upon getting them from their food.

Minerals are also needed to maintain good health. Calcium and phosphorus (along with vitamin D) are essential for bone and teeth development.

Most of the higher quality dog foods have enough vitamins and minerals added to meet your Boston terriers' needs. Supplementation, if necessary, is best done under the supervision of your veterinarian.

If you have a question about the nutritional content of a particular brand of dog food, you will find that the labels of most brands include a customer-service phone number you can call. A company representative will be happy to answer any questions you may have about the product, as well as your pet's dietary needs.

Now that you know a bit about canine nutrition you can try to evaluate the suitability of a given brand of dog food for your Boston terrier. You *must* read the labels. Keep in mind that the ingredients in dog food are listed in order of their percentage by weight. What this means is that the ingredient that makes up the bulk of the food is listed first, the next second, and so on.

What Do the Ingredients Mean?

Meat: Meat is the clean flesh of slaughtered animals. If a dog food uses a specific type of meat it will say so. Generally, the meat used in dog food is not the same that humans eat, but is rather what is left over after the cuts preferred by people are taken. This can include gristly ends and tags of striated skeletal muscle, tongue, heart, etc.

Meat by-products: These are clean animal parts other than muscle. The term can include lungs, spleen, kidneys, brain, blood, etc. However, meat by-products should not include hair, horns, teeth, and hooves.

Meat meal and meat-and-bone meal: These are made of muscle and bone tissue that has been cooked (or *rendered)* and ground. It cannot contain blood, fur, hooves, horns, hide, manure, stomach and rumen contents, or any extraneous materials. It is allowed to contain 14 percent or less of undigestible material, such as bone meal.

Poultry by-product meal: This usually consists of clean parts of the birds, such as the neck, feet, undeveloped eggs, intestines, etc., which have been rendered and ground. Poultry by-product meal should not contain feathers.

Animal by-product meal: This can be made from any animal parts except hair, hooves, horns, hide, manure, stomach and rumen contents, or any other extraneous material.

Beef tallow: Tallow is another name for fat.

Soybean meal: Soybean meal is made from the soybean flakes that are left over after oil is extracted from the beans. It is a protein source.

Brewer's rice: These are the fragments of rice left over from the milling process.

Wheat middlings: These are fragments left over from flour production.

Corn gluten meal: This is what is left over after the starch, germ, and bran are removed from the corn. It is a good source of protein.

Ground corn: This is meal made from whole-kernel corn.

Ground grain sorghum: Sorghum is a major human food crop in Africa. In this country it is primarily used as an animal feed.

Beet pulp: This is the residue from sugar beets. It is a good source of fiber.

Cereal food fines: These are fragments of breakfast cereals.

Dried kelp: Kelp is a type of seaweed. It is a source of fiber and minerals.

Selecting a Dog Food

There are a number of reasons why you should only consider buying a premium food for your Boston terrier. An important characteristic of such a product is that the contents will remain consistent from batch to batch. Producers of lower-quality dog foods cannot guarantee that the food you purchase will have the same ingredients four months from now as it has today. This is because the producers purchase ingredients in bulk on the spot market, buying whatever is a good deal at the time. Because availability depends upon such factors as weather, what is harvested at a given time of year, market conditions, and so on, they never know what will be on the market. Therefore, one item may be the primary ingredient for one batch and a different one for another. Premium dog foods are prepared according to an unvarying formula, so they will always taste and look the same.

Premium dog food should not include soybean meal, soy flour, or corn-gluten meal as its main or secondary source of protein. Nor should dog food contain a great deal of meat-and-bone meal. A better ingredient would be meat meal or poultry-by-product meal.

For more information about dog food, go to your local library and read a copy of the Association of American Feed Control Officials (AAFCO). This is a complete listing of ingredients and their definitions, as well as pet-food regulations.

Feeding Your Boston Terrier

Remember, it is up to you to determine the quality of the food you feed your dog.

Types of Dog Food

As noted above, different types of food contain different amounts of moisture. Canned food has the most water added to the food, so in essence you are paying for water. Dry food has the least amount of water, and semi-moist is in between.

While the cost of the food is not always an indication of quality, better-quality foods usually end up costing less per serving, because the dog does not need to eat as much. Some dog foods are priced in the super-premium range, but their ingredients actually place them in the premium level, so read the labels carefully.

Although the quality of the dog food is important, it is also necessary that your Boston terrier like the food. Because there are so many good-quality dog foods available, it should be a simple matter of trying out different brands to see which one your dog eats best.

One of the nicer aspects of feeding your dog an easily digestible food is that the dog will need to eat less and will therefore have less to eliminate. Some foods are loaded with red dye, sugar, or fiber and actually act as diuretics and laxatives, which can cause young dogs to have housebreaking difficulties.

At various times throughout your dog's life you will need to reevaluate the diet to determine whether it is providing the proper balance of nutrients (see page 35). As your dog becomes older, its dietary needs will change. Fortunately, if you choose a premium-quality food, the manufacturer will usually offer a variety of formulas for dogs of different ages.

You can use puppy food for your Boston terrier until it reaches maturity, at which point you can start using a maintenance-level food designed for young to middle-aged adults. As your pet gets older you can either continue with the adult food or, if you and your veterinarian think it's appropriate, you can switch to a light formula. This will ensure that your pet gets the best possible food throughout its life.

Another possibility is to cook your own dog food. As people become more health conscious, opting to make their own meals from "scratch" rather than purchasing prepared foods, they sometimes decide to extend the practice to their pets. However, experts generally advise against this, as it can be difficult to maintain the correct balance of essential ingredients needed to keep your dog healthy. Also, as your dog's needs change, you must reevaluate the contents of your homemade food.

Snacks

Many people like to give their dogs snacks or treats. There are many such items on the market. Generally, for a small dog like the Boston terrier, you should be very careful *not* to allow your dog to have many snacks. If everyone in a large household gave their dog one or two snacks each day, the total could add up to more than the entire day's ration. Many breeders and pet owners will not allow snacks at all. Some permit treats only as a reward during training or as bait in the breed ring.

Table scraps generally fall into the snack category because they are not the main source of the dog's food. Some people will not allow table scraps or any type of "people food" at all. Others will permit table scraps only in moderation. If your dog is very active, a small treat once a day or so will do no harm. However, as your Boston terrier gets older, it may not be able to burn up extra calories added to the diet in the form of snacks.

If you decide to feed your pet commercially prepared dog treats, be sure to study the labels as carefully as you would for the primary food. It is unwise to be selective about your dog's main food and then feed it lesser-quality snacks.

Feeding the Puppy

Because puppies grow fastest during the first six to eight months of their life, they need a food that is specifically designed to meet their growing needs. Most puppy foods will do this. Some people like to keep their pet on puppy food until it is a year old. However, if you notice that your puppy is getting too fat, you must either cut back on the amount of food consumed, increase its exercise, or switch to an adult maintenance food. It is a good idea to consult your veterinarian before you make any changes in your puppy's diet.

Feeding the Adult Dog

When your Boston puppy is full grown, you can switch to one of the adult maintenance foods. These are designed for the average adult pet who gets a fair amount of exercise. Because each animal is different, you must observe how much your dog eats and adjust the quantity so that it will not put on too much weight.

The key at all times is to watch your pet closely. A dog that is under a great deal of stress, or is very active physically, may need a *performance* level food that is designed for the working dog. However, if you try a performance food, watch closely to be sure that your pet does not start to gain too much weight.

Feeding the Older Dog

Often, as a dog ages, it becomes less active. Its metabolism slows down and its organ functions may become less efficient. This can hinder the dog's ability to digest food. Senior-formula dog foods are designed to compensate for this by offering highly digestible food which is lower in protein and fat.

The older your dog gets the more important it is to regulate its weight and food intake. A quality diet throughout the dog's life can add years of healthy living for your pet.

Changing Brands of Food

Sometimes it is necessary to change from one brand of food to another. Your veterinarian may recommend this because your dog has developed an allergy to a certain type of food, or, as noted above, the nutritional needs of your pet may change as it gets older.

Generally, it is not a good idea to change foods often. Before you do so, give the matter some serious thought, and always discuss it with your veterinarian. If you find that you must change dog food, introduce the new brand gradually into your pet's diet. A sudden change of food may result in digestive upsets, including diarrhea. Start by adding 20 percent of the new food to 80 percent of the old. In succeeding days increase the percentage of new food. You should allow a week or more for the changeover.

Grooming Your Boston Terrier

Grooming the Boston terrier is a rather easy task. Fancy tools and techniques are not required. For your pet, grooming will mean only regular brushing and an occasional bath. Since the Boston's coat is so short, you can wipe the dog down with a damp towel should it get soiled while playing outside. The show dog will need a little more care, but nothing elaborate is required.

It is a good idea to have a full grooming session with your dog at least once a week, in the course of which you should brush its coat, and check its ears, nails, teeth, and eyes. By giving your pet a weekly going over, you will be more likely to spot any developing problems such as lumps, bumps, and scrapes. You will also find any ticks or fleas that may have been picked up.

The Coat

A Boston terrier's coat is smooth, bright, and fine in texture. A healthy diet and a little care on your part will keep it that way.

The main grooming tool for the coat is a brush. It should have medium to soft bristles, so that you do not hurt the dog. Natural bristles will work best with the Boston terrier.

It is important to introduce your dog to the grooming routine early in life. Generally, you should start about a week after you bring your pet home. Put it on a table or other raised place, such as a bench, countertop, or grooming table. Always have a hand on the dog so that it cannot jump from the table and injure itself. Run the brush over the dog's body, petting and talking to it all the while. Stroke with the hair, not against it. Be careful not to push the brush down too hard or you could hurt your dog. Do not neglect the ears, feet, toes, and tail area. You should brush the dog at least every other day, and each grooming session should not take more then 15 minutes.

If your dog does not like to be handled, give it a treat each time you touch sensitive areas. Gradu-ally, make the dog let you handle more body areas to earn the treat. Eventually, your pet should relax.

If you plan to enter your Boston terrier in a conformation show, it will need a little extra grooming. The dogs must be trimmed for the breed ring. The idea is to enhance the dog's appearance while giving the impression that it has not been trimmed at all.

If you've never groomed a dog for show, it would be a wise idea to enlist the help of a professional groomer, but if you feel able, you can do the job yourself.

The Boston terrier should look sleek, so you will want to trim any hairs that detract from that look. This will include clipping, with as short a pair of scissors as possible, all of the coarse whiskers on the muzzle and eyebrows. Any other long hairs, such as those found on the cheek moles and the feelers under the jaw, should be trimmed as well. Other areas that usually need trimming include the backs of the front and rear legs and alongside the neck. You can use fine thinning shears for this. These shears can also be used to trim any areas of the dog's coat that seem overly heavy or thick.

After the dog is trimmed, a whitener such as chalk or talc can be rubbed into the white areas of its coat, and then rubbed out to give a good finish. After that, a coat shiner can be rubbed into the colored parts to give it an overall sheen.

The Nails

Your Boston terrier's nails should be kept very trim and not be so long as to catch your eye when you look at the feet. If you keep the nails trimmed, the *quick* (the part that bleeds) will stay back at the nail base and not grow forward. If you neglect the nails, the quick will grow, and you will have to trim the nails diligently to get the quick to recede again.

There are two styles of nail clipper on the market. One is a guillotine type, which has two

Grooming Your Boston Terrier

Use a guillotine-type nail trimmer or specially designed scissors with rounded blades. Be careful not to cut into the "quick," or bleeding will occur.

opposed blades between which you insert the nail. Then, a squeeze of a lever chops off the nail. The second type is a scissors with rounded blades. Neither type gives inferior service, so the choice is purely a matter of personal preference.

Be sure to check your dogs ear periodically.

You should keep *styptic* powder handy to stop bleeding when it occurs. This powder can be purchased at any pet-supply store. Another useful tool is a nail file, which can be used after clipping the nails to smooth sharp edges.

How often you need to trim the nails will depend upon your pet's lifestyle. If it runs daily on pavement, its nails will tend to wear down naturally and you may only have to trim them once every week or two. If your pet spends most of its time on carpeted floors, you will need to trim the nails more often. Also, a dog's nails will grow at different rates depending upon its health and age.

The Ears

By checking your dog's ears on a regular basis you will catch any problems while they are still developing. Look for excessive wax, inflammation, or a strong, foul odor. Frequent head-shaking or pain when the dog's ears are touched or scratched warrant an immediate trip to the veterinarian.

You should check your pet's ears at least once a week. If you notice a wax buildup, you can clean them out with a special preparation, which you can purchase from your veterinarian or pet-supply store. Alternatively, your veterinarian may tell you how to clean your pet's ears using household products.

Never put anything in your dog's ears without checking with your veterinarian first.

The Teeth

It is important to brush your dog's teeth on a regular basis. If you start when your pet is a puppy, it will learn to enjoy the attention. You must use a baby toothbrush, or one that was designed for canine use. Use a special canine toothpaste, which is available from your veterinarian or local pet-supply store. You should *never* use human toothpaste for a dog, as it is toxic.

Grooming Your Boston Terrier

When brushing your dog's teeth, be sure to clean all surfaces—top, bottom, inside, outside, front, and back. Brush the teeth in the same pattern as you would brush your own. Always brush from gum to tooth tip, so you do not push any tartar under the gums.

If your dog will allow you to do so, you can floss its teeth as well.

Some dogs will not permit their teeth to be brushed. There are also finger toothbrushes that work well. If your pet is like this, you can rub its teeth with baking soda or canine toothpaste, and a soft cloth. This will help to keep your dog's breath smelling nice.

You should take your pet to the veterinarian periodically to have its teeth cleaned. If you notice bad breath not caused by eating something which has a foul odor, you should go in for a check-up. Persistent bad breath in dogs usually indicates that it has oral disease.

Dogs, just like people, are subject to gum diseases and infections. If left untreated, these can lead to serious complications.

The Eyes

Your dog's eyes should not require special care. However, if you go walking in an area of high weeds or brush, you should check your pet's eyes afterward to see if any seeds or pollen are causing irritation. The dog will show signs of irritation by pawing at the eyes, excessive watering, or persistent blinking.

If you suspect that there is something in the dog's eyes, rinse them with warm water. *Do not try to pull back the eyelids to check the eyes.* If the problem does not resolve within an hour or so you should call your veterinarian. Yellow or green mucus discharge from the eyes is a sign of possible infection; you should consult your veterinarian without delay.

Odor

Although Boston terriers do not usually have a strong odor, you will sometimes notice a foul or musky scent about your dog. Generally, a bath will not solve this problem. The odor is caused by secretions from the *anal sacs,* located just below the tail on the inside of the rectum.

Some of the odorous fluid can be expressed by periodically depressing the anal sacs. Your veterinarian can do this for you, and a good groomer will do it as part of a routine grooming session (be sure to ask). Or you can learn to do the job yourself. Dogs who are more active are less likely to require expression of their sacs; older and less active dogs may need to be checked more often. Generally you should not need to do this with a puppy.

Depressing the anal sacs is not something you want to do too often, since it can cause irritation and infection. However, should they become blocked, which happens occasionally, have them cleaned out by your veterinarian.

The Bath

While it should not be necessary to bathe your Boston terrier often, there are times when you will need to do it.

Before you start your dog's bath, be sure to take it for a walk so its bladder will be empty. Otherwise, the warm water of the bath may make your dog feel the urge to urinate.

Be sure to have everything ready for the bath before you start. You will want a bathmat, shampoo, towels, a face cloth, and a spray hose or container you can use to wet your dog down.

Initially the dog may not like the bath. It is always amazing how our dogs love to wallow in muddy puddles but hate a clean bath! If your pet fights you to the point where you cannot give the bath, you will need to get help from a friend.

Because the Boston terrier is small, you can bathe it almost anywhere in your house. A bathtub, kitchen sink, or laundry tub will do. You should have a rubber bathmat for your pet to stand on. This will give the dog traction and help to keep it from slipping.

There are many shampoos on the market formulated specifically for dogs. Most of them are fine and will do a good job. Always use a shampoo that is mild and safe for dogs. Since you will not bathe your dog often there should be no need to use a conditioner on its coat.

Begin the bath by thoroughly wetting the dog with warm water. Start wetting from the head and work down to the tail. Be careful to keep water out of the eyes and ears. You may find that the oils in the dog's coat cause water to roll off and not really get to the skin. Do not worry about this. If you know how, this is a good time to depress the anal sacs.

Next, being careful not to get soap in your dog's eyes or nose, lather the dog with your dog shampoo. Take some of the suds and rub them on the face. You can use a cloth to wash the dog's face to avoid getting soap in the eyes and nose. Work back from the neck to the tail, making sure that you soap the underside, as well as the legs and feet, including the toes.

Always watch for fleas as you give your dog a bath. By bathing the dog from the head to the tail you will force any fleas to migrate to the rump. From there they can be washed away. If you work from the tail to the head the fleas will run into your pet's ears, eyes, and nose.

When your dog is completely soaped, you can start rinsing. Again, start from the head and work toward the tail. When you have finished rinsing, run your hands all over the dog's body, including its underside, to feel if you've missed any soap.

Towel dry your dog. It is not a good idea to use blow driers designed for humans, because they tend to dry out the coat and can burn the skin. There are professional machines designed for dogs, but you will most likely find that a towel gives perfectly good results.

Keep your dog indoors for a few hours after the bath, so it can dry off completely. This will also prevent your dog from running outside to roll in the dirt because it does not like the smell of the shampoo you used.

Always be extra kind to your dog when giving it a bath. Young puppies might be frightened by the experience, and need reassurance and praise for putting up with their first bath. You can give your pet little treats during the bathing process to reward good behavior.

You should avoid bathing puppies if at all possible. But if you must, consult with your veterinarian as to what product you should use. This is an absolute must if you find it necessary to give your puppy a bath with a flea shampoo. Many flea products which are fine for adult dogs are not safe to use on puppies.

If you have practiced handling your dog and putting it in the bathing area, you should not have a great deal of trouble. As a final word of caution, do not let your dog drink the soapy water. It can make your dog sick if it drinks enough of it. Remember that little dogs do not need much to make them sick.

Medical Considerations

Choosing a Veterinarian

Before you bring your new pet home, you should have already chosen a veterinarian. Some of the criteria you can use to help you choose a veterinarian follow.

1. Ask friends who own dogs who they use and how they like their veterinarians.
2. Ask other professionals, such as your local groomer, dog trainer, boarding-kennel operator, or pet shop to make recommendations.
3. Go to all the nearby veterinary clinics, explain that you are getting a new dog, and ask to see the facilities and meet the doctor.
4. Determine which clinic has hours that suit your schedule, and find out if it maintains 24-hour emergency coverage.
5. If the clinic uses an emergency service, find out where it is located, as it may be too far away to be able to handle a real crisis situation.
6. Ask each clinic how much the basic office visit costs, as well as some other charges, such as spaying and neutering, shots, teeth-cleaning, etc.
7. Find out how many veterinarians work at the clinic. (You may prefer the security of knowing that a larger clinic is open longer hours and has someone on call; or you may opt for a smaller office where you always can be seen by the same person.)

The answers to these questions may help you to determine which veterinary clinic to choose.

An Ounce of Prevention...

There are many things you can do to keep your Boston terrier healthy and happy. Accidents harm and kill more dogs each year than people realize. Just think of how many dead dogs you see lying along the roadside. Before you allow your Boston

Next to you, your veterinarian can be your dog's best friend. Short visits just to say "Hi" and to receive a special treat will help make future visits easier.

terrier to engage in any activity, think of things which could possibly go wrong.

Do not let your dog play off the leash near major roads, or in areas adjacent to traffic unless the area is securely fenced. If the area in question is a public place, be sure to walk the fence line to look for any openings through which a small dog could escape. Even the most obedient dog will disobey occasionally, and all you need is one accident to ruin or even end your pet's life.

If you want to allow your dog to try swimming, be sure that the water is safe. You must consider the current, both on and under the surface. Even with a mild current, a Boston terrier could easily be swept away. Unlike water dogs, such as Labrador retrievers, Bostons are not strong swimmers. You must also be concerned about possible toxic substances in the water. All dogs drink some water as they swim.

Medical Considerations

Toxic Plants and Plant Parts

Anemone	Holly berries	Narcissus
Angel's trumpet tree	Horsetail reed	Nightshade
Apricot kernels	Hyacinth	Oleander
Arrowhead	Hydrangea	Periwinkle
Avocado leaves	Iris	Peyote (mescal)
Azaleas	Ivy (Boston, English, and	Philodendron
Betel nut	others)	Poison hemlock
Palm	Jack-in-the-Pulpit	Poison ivy
Bittersweet	Jequirity bean	Poison oak
Buckeye	Jerusalem cherry	Poppy (California poppy
Buttercup	Jessamine (jasmine)	excepted)
Caladium	Jimson weed (thorn apple)	Pokeweed
Calla lily	Jonquil	Potato sprouts
Castor bean	Lantana camara (red sage)	Primrose
Cherries (wild and cultivated)	Larkspur	Ranunculus
Crocus	Laurel	Rhododendron
Daffodil	Lily-of-the-valley	Rhubarb blade
Daphne	Lobelia	Rosary pea
Delphinium	Marijuana	Star-of-Bethlehem
Devil's ivy	Mayapple	Sweet pea
Dieffenbachia (dumb cane)	Mistletoe	Tobacco
Elderberry	Moonseed	Tomato vine
Elephant ear	Monkshood	Tulip
English ivy	Morning glory	Water hemlock
Four-o'clock	Mother-in-law plant	Wisteria
Foxglove	Mushroom	Yew

If you are going to allow your dog to run in the woods, be on the lookout for leg-hold traps that have been placed on animal runs. You should also carry a first-aid kit to care for bee stings, snake bites, cuts and scrapes.

If you are hiking in the woods in certain parts of the country, beware of old wells and holes into which a small dog could fall. By keeping your dog on a leash or in your sight, you will prevent most of these types of accidents from happening. Think before you allow your dog to do *anything*.

Prevention should be the watchword for your home as well. Toxic plants occur inside and out-side the home; be sure that all dangerous plants are out of chewing range for your dog. Check with your veterinarian, poison control center or local extension agent to determine which toxic plants are found in your area. Even though young

Praise and consistency are the keys to proper training and good performance in the obedience ring. Obviously, both the Boston terrier and its proud mistress enjoy demonstrating the "Heel" (top left), the "Come" (top right), and the "Figure 8 heel" (bottom).

Medical Considerations

Plants Considered to be Nontoxic

Abelia
Abyssinian sword lily
African daisy
African palm
African violet
Airplane plant
Aluminum plant
Aralia
Aracucaria (may cause dermatitis)
Aspidistra (cast iron plant)
Aster
Baby's tears
Bachelor button
Bamboo
Begonia
Birds nest fern
Blood leaf plant
Boston fern
Bougainvillea
Cactus (certain varieties)
California holly
California poppy
Camellia
Christmas cactus

Coleus
Corn plant
Crab apple
Creeping Charlie
Creeping Jennie,
  moneywort, lysima
Croton (house variety)
Dahlia
Daisy
Dandelion
Dogwood
Donkey tail
Dracaena
Echeveria
Eucalyptus (caution; can
  be toxic to some dogs)
Eugenia
Gardenia
Grape ivy
Hedge apple
Hens and chicks
Honeysuckle
Hoya
Jade plant

Kalanchoe
Lily (day, Easter, or tiger)
Lipstick plant
Magnolia
Marigold
Monkey plant
Mother-in-law's tongue
Norfolk island pine
Peperomia
Petunia
Prayer plant
Purple passion
Pyracantha
Rose
Sansevieria
Scheffelera
Sensitive plant
Spider plant
Swedish ivy
Umbrella plant
Violet
Wandering Jew
Weeping willow
Zebra plant

puppies are more likely to chew plants and chemicals than adults, an older dog can be counted on to occasionally chew something it should not. If your dog happens to eat a toxic plant you should call your veterinarian or poison-control center right away. Do not wait for symptoms to develop.

Communication is essential to forming a good bond with your pet. A young woman talks to her dog while waiting their turn in the obedience ring (top), demonstrates the "Heel" (bottom left), and then offers praise for a job well done (bottom right).

The above plants are considered to be nontoxic. However, any plant can cause an unexpected reaction in a given individual. If your dog eats one of these plants watch carefully for a day, but generally there will be no need to become alarmed.

If your dog should eat a plant that you are not sure of, take a sample of it to your local garden center for identification, or call your veterinarian. Bear in mind that weed killers can be much more harmful to dogs than the plants themselves. Also, be careful of fertilizers, both for outdoor and indoor use. Most chemical fertilizers are toxic to animals.

Medical Considerations

Boston terriers, being small animals, are low to the ground and can breathe in significant quantities of weed killer and fertilizer. Dogs have been known to get sick from eating grass treated with liquid chemicals. Check with the manufacturer and your veterinarian before using any of these chemicals around your pet.

Rodent poisons are another concern. While some require a number of ingestions to kill a dog, you should still call your veterinarian immediately if you suspect that your dog has eaten some.

Immunizations

As a responsible owner, it will be important to properly take care of the health of your dog. Part of this care includes regular vaccinations. Timely inoculations can prevent many serious diseases, some of which can be deadly.

During the first year of your dog's life it will need to get a series of inoculations, after which yearly boosters will keep its immunity at an acceptable level. You can expect the schedule for shots to be something like this:

- Six weeks: canine distemper
- Eight weeks: canine distemper, hepatitis, leptospirosis, parainfluenza, parvovirus (DHLPP); Bordetella and coronavirus vaccinations may also be recommended.
- Twelve weeks: DHLPP, and heartworm preventive medication if advised by your veterinarian; Bordetella and coronavirus vaccinations may also be recommended.
- Sixteen weeks: DHLPP and rabies; Bordetella and coronavirus vaccinations may also be recommended.

If you live in an area where your dog will be walking in grass, woods, or fields, you may want to consider a vaccination against Lyme disease.

After the initial inoculations your dog should only need a yearly booster and an annual test for heartworms.

Some Serious Diseases

Canine distemper: This virus is the leading infectious cause of death in dogs. Symptoms resemble the common cold in humans. The dog's eyes will be watery and its nose will run. Next, usually within days, the discharge will turn thick yellow. The dog will then develop a fever, become listless, and not want to eat. Seizures are late symptoms, and death frequently results. Sometimes a dog can appear to recover, only to experience a lethal relapse.

Distemper is not limited to dogs and can be found in other small mammals. The disease is often found in puppies, but adults can catch it too if they have not had their annual booster vaccinations. It is not unusual for a whole litter of puppies to die of distemper.

Leptospirosis: These bacteria are usually found in the urine of an infected animal. Your dog can become infected by drinking, swimming, or wading in infected water, and by eating infected food. Due to improved sanitation practices and widespread inoculation, this disease is no longer common. However, it can be transmitted to humans.

Signs of leptospirosis are loss of appetite, diarrhea, and fever. It can cause permanent damage to the liver and kidneys. The dog can become jaundiced, weak in the hind legs, develop sores in the mouth, and suffer from abdominal pain.

Canine hepatitis: This is a highly contagious disease which usually strikes quickly. Although it can be mild, severe cases can cause quick death in dogs. If left untreated, the virus will attack the liver, kidneys, and the lining of the blood vessels.

The signs of hepatitis are listlessness, fever, tonsillitis, bloody stools, abdominal pain, and vomiting.

Canine Parvoviral Disease: This is a highly contagious disease transmitted by infected feces. Canine parvoviral disease can strike dogs of all ages, but has a very high mortality rate for puppies of five months and less.

Medical Considerations

There are two major types of canine parvoviral disease; both are highly contagious and often fatal. One form affects the dog's heart muscles. A puppy will stop nursing, cry, and have difficulty breathing. Very shortly, it will die. The other form causes a high fever, depression, loss of appetite, extreme pain, vomiting, and very extreme bloody diarrhea. These last symptoms will cause dehydration. There will be little or no urine output; and the nose, mouth and eyes will be dry. If the puppy is treated quickly by a veterinarian there is a good chance of survival.

Coronavirus: This, too, is a very contagious disease that attacks puppies and unvaccinated dogs. It is often misdiagnosed as parvovirus because of the similarity of its signs: a very bad, foul-smelling, and occasionally bloody diarrhea. Dehydration is a problem with this disease, and you should isolate your dog and immediately take it to your veterinarian.

Rabies: All warm-blooded animals, including man, are susceptible to rabies. The disease is transmitted through the saliva of an infected animal. Rabies causes the brain to become inflamed, which will cause altered behavior and neurological function. Some of the signs are withdrawal, paralysis, and erratic violent behavior.

Rabies is endemic and widespread. Every year rabid animals are reported throughout the country. If you see a mammal of any species acting strangely, do not attempt to catch it yourself. Instead, call the proper animal-control authorities. They will catch the animal, and either quarantine it to see if it develops rabies, or else destroy it.

As long as your Boston terrier is not exposed to wildlife (including mice) there is no great danger to either you or the dog. If your pet should be bitten by a wild animal, immediately call your veterinarian to treat the wound and take precautionary measures against rabies. Up-to-date vaccines, required for license renewal in most areas, are the best prevention.

Parainfluenza: This virus causes infectious tracheobronchitis and is very contagious, especially when groups of dogs are kept close together. Because of its frequent appearance in group settings, the disease has been nicknamed "kennel cough." However, your dog can catch it just as easily from an encounter with a single infected animal.

Signs are a dry, hacking cough which, if left untreated, will be followed by retching to get rid of mucus in the throat. In and of itself, this disease is not life-threatening. The danger lies in increased vulnerability to other infections and ailments.

Bordetella: Bordetella is a bacterial infection that causes symptoms similar to the parainfluenza virus, and may also be referred to as infectious tracheobronchitis. Severe cases can cause bronchopneumonia. Annual vaccination is recommended.

Lyme disease (Spirochaetosis): Like rabies, Lyme disease can affect all warm-blooded animals, including man. It is transmitted by the deer tick. Because these ticks are about the size of a pinhead, they are almost impossible to spot, making prevention the best course. If you live in an infested area, and you plan to walk, hike, or otherwise spend any amount of time outdoors with your dog, you should take precautions.

The symptoms of Lyme disease can vary from case to case. Many times, when either you or your dog is bitten by an infected tick, the bite will swell or there may be a painless red rash. However, the rash may not appear, and it can be small and easily missed. Later symptoms of Lyme disease can include arthritic swelling and tenderness of the joints. If treated right away, it is possible to cure the dog and yourself, but delay in treatment can lead to difficulties.

The easiest way to protect both yourself and your dog is to use a tick-repellant spray. The problem with this method is that the dog will probably lick the spray off, nullifying its usefulness and allowing your dog to ingest some toxic material. After your walk you can use a flea comb to check your pet. A good precaution for your dog is a Lyme-disease injection.

Lyme disease was discovered fairly recently and scientists are continuing to gain knowledge about it. Therefore, you would be wise to keep in touch with your veterinarian to get the latest information.

Internal Parasites

Dogs are afflicted by a number of species of parasitic worms. Almost all puppies have worms, and adult dogs can pick them up too. Wormy puppies will not thrive, and in both puppies and adult dogs, worms can cause serious health problems and death.

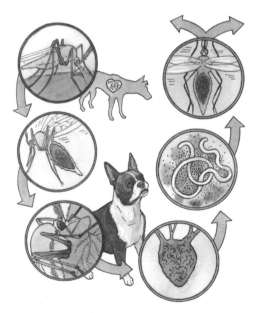

Carried to the dog by mosquitos, heartworm is one of the most preventable of parasites. Without preventive medication, the larvae mature in the dog's heart.

Some worms can be detected by microscopic examination of the feces, while others are found in the blood. In some cases you can actually see the worms around the dog's anus or in its stool.

You should never consider worming your pet without consulting your veterinarian. Worming medications are formulated for use against specific worms, so proper diagnosis is essential. Over-the-counter medications might not be effective against your pet's worms, and some can actually cause harm. The same is true of homemade worming preparations or remedies.

You should have your dog checked for worms at least twice a year—when it gets its annual booster shots and then six months later. To do this, take a fresh stool sample with you for examination. This will ensure that your dog is free of these pesky internal parasites.

If your dog should get worms it is important to keep your living area and the places where the dog eliminates very clean, so that it will not become reinfected. Some worms are eliminated in the dog's stools, and will survive in the ground for a long time. Check with your veterinarian as to the best way to disinfect your dog's toilet area.

As a general rule of thumb you should look at your dog's stools daily when they are fresh to check for worms, blood, mucus, color, and consistency. Often this is the only way you can spot the early warning signs of disease or infestations in your dog.

Roundworms: These are most often found in puppies. If the mother has roundworms they can be transmitted to the puppies before birth or during nursing. In fact, all puppies should be assumed to have worms and, therefore, should be wormed twice; once before leaving the breeder's kennel, and again two weeks later. Infected puppies will not look as healthy as puppies who do not have the worms. Sometimes they will vomit worms up, or they may pass in the stools. One of the signs in an infested puppy is a big, round pot belly. Your veterinarian can examine the puppy to determine if it has worms.

Medical Considerations

Heartworm: These round worms are parasitic on dogs, cats, and ferrets. The larvae are transmitted by mosquitoes and live under the dog's skin for two or three months. Then they mature into worms and travel through the bloodstream to the heart and lungs. They can live there for up to five years and grow from 4 to 12 inches long. They wrap themselves around the heart valves and can cause heart failure and death.

The effects of heartworm do not show until years after the initial infection. The major symptoms are a dry, soft cough, and an inability to tolerate exercise. Later complications can involve the heart, liver, and kidneys.

Heartworm is one of the most easily preventable of canine diseases. If you live in a region where the disease is endemic, you can give your dog a daily or a monthly preventive medication, which can be obtained from your veterinarian.

Hookworms: These can be present in both adult dogs and puppies. Hookworm eggs are passed on through the infected animal's stool. The eggs hatch into larvae, which attach themselves to the feet of the same or another dog and penetrate the skin. Larvae can also be swallowed with food, water, or even inhaled when a contaminated area is sniffed. As with roundworm infestation, puppies who have hookworms will not thrive. The stool will be bloody or inky, the pups will not maintain their weight, and they may not eat well. If left untreated for a long period, hookworms can cause the development of scar tissue in the intestines, which will cause chronic intestinal problems for the rest of the dog's life. Because hookworms attach themselves to the intestinal wall and suck blood, your puppy can develop anemia and could die.

In clean surroundings hookworm infestation is rare. Therefore, breeders and owners should maintain meticulously sanitary conditions. However, if you walk your dog in areas where many animals have been (such as the exercise pen at a dog show), your pet can get hookworms regardless of how clean you keep your home area.

Tapeworms: Tapeworms are long flatworms that can be acquired by many kinds of animals, including humans. They consist of a head, which attaches to the intestinal wall, and a large number of sections. Each section is filled with eggs, and has the capacity to become a new tapeworm. When the segments are ready, they pass out of the dog in the stool.

There are several species of tapeworms, each with a different life cycle. Fleas are the principal intermediate host for the Dipylidium tapeworm in dogs. Fleas ingest the tapeworm eggs that have been passed in the dog's feces, and the tapeworm eggs develop into cysts inside the flea. If the flea jumps on a dog and the dog happens to swallow the flea, the dog becomes infected with the tapeworm. Farm animals such as sheep, cattle, and pigs can serve as intermediate hosts for the Echinococeus

The tapeworm cycle: the flea can be a host for tapeworm eggs. Eggs, transmitted to the dog, mature into tapeworms. Tapeworm segments, some of which are passed in the feces, release more eggs. Other types of tapeworm eggs also can be found in raw fish or meat.

tapeworm. The farm animals get the tapeworms from grazing in areas infected by dog's droppings and the dogs get the tapeworm from eating the offal of an infected animal.

Although not life-threatening, tapeworms can cause general poor health in your dog. If a tapeworm is present, you will usually see segments hanging from the hairs around the dog's anus or in the stools. Sometimes the worm can pass in very long segments and appear as white or grey strings which your dog strains to eliminate. Your veterinarian, who can examine stool samples for tapeworm eggs, can also provide you with effective medication.

Whipworms: Generally, whipworms affect dogs over six months of age. Some dogs can have whipworms with no side effects; others can develop foul smelling diarrhea, which can become a problem.

Because whipworm eggs have a very thick shell, it is possible for them to lie dormant for years. This can make it very difficult to clean an infected area.

The larvae develop inside the egg and stay there until conditions are right for them to hatch. The dog picks up the eggs on its paws when it walks on contaminated ground. When the dog licks its paws the eggs are injested. They hatch in the small intestines, then move to the large intestines. Finally, they are passed with the feces, and the cycle starts all over again.

A dog can also pick up whipworm eggs if it eats contaminated dirt.

External Parasites

Fleas: These are perhaps the most troublesome of the external parasites. Fleas feed on the dog's blood and can cause anemia. They also transmit tapeworms. Some Boston terriers can develop a flea allergy, which will cause hair loss, constant scratching, and skin problems.

The only way to prevent fleas is to establish an aggressive flea-killing and prevention program. You must attack fleas at all stages of their development, both on your dog and in its environment.

You cannot control fleas in your house simply by giving your dog a flea bath. You must treat the whole house with products that kill immature fleas before they can reproduce, as well as give your dog periodic baths until the fleas are under control. When using flea baths, powders and sprays, read the manufacturer's directions carefully and follow them explicitly. Until you kill every flea that has hatched in your house, which takes several weeks, you will not get rid of the infestation.

It is not a good idea to use a flea collar on your dog because it will not kill the fleas living in your house. Because Boston terriers are a small breed, you must be concerned about toxic buildup in their systems as a result of flea products you might use. You should consult your veterinarian as to what to do.

If you have more than one dog, the battle against fleas will be more difficult. If you have a severe problem you may need to call an exterminator.

Ticks: These are also blood suckers, and certain species can transmit disease, including Lyme disease. Ticks usually do not attach themselves to your dog right away, so if you go out in areas which may be infested, check your dog as soon as you come home, and you may be able to pick off any ticks before they embed.

If you find that a tick has attached itself to your dog, take it off making sure not to leave any mouthparts behind. Clean the bite and put on a first aid cream. Then bring the tick to your veterinarian right away for identification.

To remove a tick, first wipe the area with alcohol. This will loosen the tick's grasp. Next, place a pair of tweezers directly over the head of the tick as close to the dog's skin as possible. Carefully grasp the tick's body and lift it off the dog. Try not to pull the body apart. If the head remains under the dog's skin it can cause an infection.

Once the tick is removed, either put it in a container such as a zip loc bag (to take to your veterinarian for identification) or dispose of it. However, before you dispose of a tick, make sure it is dead by placing it in a small amount of rubbing alcohol for a few minutes. Once the tick is dead, flush it down the toilet or put it in your trash. A live tick that is flushed down the toilet can survive, especially in a septic system.

Ear Mites: These parasites, which live in the ear canal, cause *otitis* (or ear inflammation) and produce a dark, waxy residue. Ear mites are transmitted from one animal to another. While they can only be seen through a microscope, you can notice a strong odor in the ear. Ear mites should be treated immediately by your veterinarian.

Mange: There are two types of mange, *demodectic,* or red mange, and *sarcoptic* mange, or scabies. Both types are caused by mites. Red mange usually affects old dogs and puppies. The dog will suffer from hair loss and sometimes itching. Scabies is a highly contagious condition transmitted by physical contact. Humans can pick up the parasite as well. Scabies causes hair loss and very bad itching. You should take your dog immediately to a veterinarian for treatment.

Other Skin Problems: Boston terriers can suffer from allergies to pollen, chemicals, flea bites, etc., and contract fungal infections.

Your dog's body changes as it ages, and it may experience reactions to irritants that never bothered it before. If you notice symptoms such as bald spots, itching, rashes, scabs from scratching, or discharges, take your pet to your veterinarian immediately .

Other Illnesses and Medical Problems

Vomiting and Diarrhea: There are a number of conditions which can cause these symptoms. Stress could be a cause, as well as eating grass, or

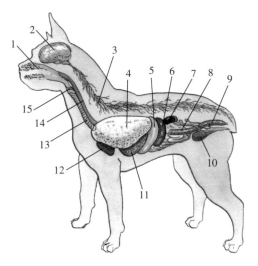

Internal anatomy of the Boston terrier: 1. Sinus cavity; 2. Brain; 3. Spinal cord; 4. Lungs; 5. Stomach; 6. Spleen; 7. Kidneys; 8. Small intestine; 9. Colon; 10. Bladder; 11. Liver; 12. Heart; 13. Trachea; 14. Esophagus; 15. Thyroid cartilage.

any change in diet. Sometimes sudden hot weather can cause a dog to drink excessively, and this can result in one or two bouts of diarrhea or vomiting. Try withdrawing all food for 12 hours. Provide small amounts of fresh water. If the symptoms are relieved, offer a small quantity of food. However, if vomiting recurs, or if vomiting or diarrhea lasts longer then 12 hours, or if there are other signs of illness, call your veterinarian without delay.

Constipation: Lack of exercise can cause constipation, even if the inactivity is due to a long trip in a confined area. If it lasts longer then a day, or if the dog is in discomfort, you should call your veterinarian.

Epilepsy: Epilepsy is a condition of recurring seizures. Different types of seizures cause different symptoms, including loss of consciousness, collapse, muscle spasms, shaking, and loss of control of the bowels and bladder. The seizure itself may often be preceded by a period of altered behavior, which can include restlessness, pacing, an abnormal need for affection, heavy salivation and drooling, shivering or shaking, and hiding. During the seizure, the dog can exhibit excitement, vomiting, salivation, and running in circles, as well as the more severe behavior mentioned above.

If your dog has what you think is a seizure, try to remove anything nearby which could hurt it, such as furniture and sharp objects. Do not put your hand in the dog's mouth. If the seizure does not end within five minutes call your veterinarian for emergency help.

Diabetes: This refers to a condition in which there is excess sugar in the circulation, caused by a decrease in the amount of effective insulin in the body. While there is no cure, it can be controlled, sometimes by diet alone, although daily injections may be required. Some of the signs are an increase in appetite and hunger, and increased urination.

Pancreatitis: This is inflammation of the pancreas, usually occurring in overweight, middle-aged female house dogs who have lived on a high-fat diet. The signs include vomiting, diarrhea, lack of appetite, depression, restlessness, and tenderness of the stomach and belly. In some cases, proper medication and diet can keep a dog alive and comfortable with pancreatitis for a long time. Acute pancreatitis requires immediate veterinary care or it may become life-threatening.

Special Considerations for the Old Dog

From about eight years of age on, various aspects of your dog's physiological function will tend to become less efficient. With a little bit of care and extra precautionary measures, you can make sure your dog has a long, healthy, and comfortable life.

Perhaps the most important factor in producing a hale and happy old age for your dog is nutrition. If you have been giving it a super-premium dog food for its entire life, your pet's overall condition will be superior.

If you notice that your older dog likes to sleep more, or is reluctant to go out on cool, damp days, you should look for weight gain. Now might be the time to put your pet on a low-calorie adult dog food.

Another important part of the care of the older dog is to give it a complete veterinary examination every year. Depending upon your dog's condition, this should include a full set of blood tests (including CBC, chemistry, and differential), a T3–T4 assay, and a urinalysis. These tests will allow your veterinarian to discover problems in their early stages, before symptoms have become evident. They will reveal the state of function of the major organs in your dog's body, the presence of infection, and much more.

Arthritis is a common problem in older dogs, and could be another reason your pet may not be as lively as previously. Now is the time to start some preventive and pain-relieving measures. Nonstrenuous exercise and antioxidant treatments are frequently successful, and in some dogs has worked wonders. Acupuncture is another way to treat arthritic pain, as well as pain from other causes.

You should only use these measures under the direction of a veterinarian who is trained in their use. To obtain a list of licensed veterinary acupuncturists, see page 82.

Breeding Your Boston Terrier

To Breed or Not To Breed?

Before you consider breeding your Boston terrier, you should think long and hard about your reasons for wanting to do so. There is only one really good reason and a number of bad ones.

To make a lot of money: For both the sire and dam there are a great deal of expenses involved in producing a litter of quality puppies. Both parents need to be genetically tested to make sure that they do not have inheritable conditions or other medical problems which could make the puppies undesirable or risk your dog's life during the birth process.

You need to determine if both are good quality. This means the dogs should possess working titles, such as obedience degrees and/or breed wins in a conformation show. And you must be sure that both dogs have good temperament. These are just a small part of what goes into proving that a dog is worthy of breeding.

The actual cost of breeding quality dogs can be very high, and if there are complications you can actually lose money.

To let the kids watch the miracle of birth and play with the puppies as they grow up: The birth process is often not pleasant to watch, and since about three quarters of all Boston terriers must be whelped by caesarean section, the kids will not get to watch it anyway.

Boston puppies are very small, and can be injured by children trying to play with them. This is especially likely if there are a number of puppies running around at the same time. It is much safer to buy a puppy and supervise the interaction between the child and that one animal, rather than having to watch a number of puppies at once.

We love our dog and want one just like it: The chances of getting puppies just like the parents are very slim. If breeders could reproduce their dogs that closely there would not be such a wide range of personalities and types within a breed. By breeding to produce a dog just like the one you have, you are putting your eggs all in one basket, so to speak. By shopping around for a Boston terrier from established breeders you will have a much better chance of finding a dog just like yours, since you will have so many to pick from. What will you do if you have a litter and none of the puppies turn out the way you had hoped? There is no way to judge what kind of adult the puppy will turn into. The only thing you can tell in that respect is the dog's color.

Everyone wants a dog just like ours: This is usually true until the time comes to *pay* for the puppy. Are you prepared to keep all of the puppies you cannot sell or give away? Are you prepared to back up the puppies you are responsible for producing? This means giving purchasers the same type of guarantee you got from your breeder when you bought your dog. And the owner of the sire of the litter is just as responsible for the well-being of the puppies as the owner of the dam.

What are you going to do when you add up the cost of breeding your dog, figure out what you need to charge for a puppy just to break even, and your friends reply, "Oh, I didn't think the puppy would cost that much," or "We just can't afford it right now." Friends usually expect great bargains from friends, and probably have no idea of the expenses involved in breeding.

We really like puppies: Well, think again. Enjoying a single puppy is one thing, but raising a whole litter is quite another. Are you prepared to bottle-feed the puppies every few hours around the clock in the event that the mother cannot or does not want to feed them? What if the mother dies?

Are you prepared to clean up after the puppies, who will make quite a mess, especially after the first few weeks.

From the time the puppies are born until they are placed in their new homes, their cleaning and feeding needs will prevent you from leaving the house for more then a few hours at a time.

Then there is the matter of properly socializing the puppies from birth until they are placed in their new home (see page 65). Once the puppies are gone you will need to be available for phone calls and questions from the new owners.

If you are the owner of the sire, are you prepared to help if the dam's owner is unable to care for the puppies? What if the whole litter is dumped on you to care for?

It is better for the bitch to have a litter before she is spayed: Actually it is healthier for your bitch to be spayed before she comes into heat for the first time. If you have her spayed at about six months of age you will significantly reduce her chances of getting mammary, uterine, or ovarian cancers. She will also be less likely to roam, and will not mess the house during her heats. You will not have to worry about an accidental pregnancy.

Having her spayed will not reduce her protective instincts, nor will it make her fat and lazy. The only reason a dog becomes obese after being spayed is because the owners give the dog extra treats and do not exercise it, thinking they should coddle her because "she has just had an operation." Special treatment following major surgery of any kind should be given according to the recommendation of your veterinarian.

It is better for a dog to be bred before I neuter (or castrate) him: This is not true for a number of reasons. First, if you neuter the male dog before he is bred it will reduce the tendency for him to wander, mark (urinate) in your house and on your property, be aggressive toward other dogs, and wander off in search of a bitch. The neutered male will be more relaxed overall, and a nicer dog to live with.

Neutering a male dog at around six months of age will reduce the chances of tumors and cancer. It will not cause the dog to become lazy or fat, and will spare you from weeks of whining and pacing every time he senses a bitch in heat in the area.

Keep in mind that the dog has no idea what has been done to him when he is neutered. He will not harbor a grudge and be mad at you because you have taken away his ability to breed. If anything, he will be a happier dog.

Yes, I Want To Breed My Boston Terrier

If, after extensive soul-searching and meticulous planning, you still feel as though you want to produce a litter of Boston terrier puppies, you should do *more* soul-searching. Bringing a litter of puppies into the world is a very serious matter. Always ask yourself why you want to raise puppies. Casual breeding is not recommended, neither for the experienced breeder nor the first timer. The cute puppies you bring into the world are your *responsibility*. You are responsible for their care, for their physical and mental well-being, and for finding each puppy a top-quality home. How would you feel if you learned a year after you sold a puppy that it was mistreated because you had misjudged your customer?

Every responsible dog breeder must take responsibility for all of their puppies for each one's entire life. How would you feel if one of your puppies came back to you in such condition that you had to have it destroyed? Never lose sight of the fact that millions of unwanted puppies are killed every year for want of a good home. These dogs are purebred, mixed breed, young and old alike. For every puppy born, one or more dogs dies because that puppy filled one of the few available pet slots that exist. That is a very sobering thought, which should weigh heavily on your conscience.

Also, consider the fact that every litter you produce shapes the destiny of the Boston terrier breed, for some of the puppies you produce will be bred as well. If you decide, after deep soul-searching, that you want to go ahead and breed your dog, you can do the best job possible by becoming a good student of the Boston terrier.

To start, you should intensively examine the breed. See what the champions are like, both in mind and body. Get to know as many Boston terrier breeders as possible. Study their dogs and their dogs' histories. Learn about dog breeding in depth. Also, give careful study to your own financial position, to be sure that you have enough money to cover worst-case scenarios. This is especially necessary if you are the owner of the bitch.

As a final test of your intentions, visit your local animal shelter and look at all the unwanted dogs. Most of them will be killed within the next few days.

Stud Dog and Bitch

There is only one good reason to breed a dog, and that is to improve the quality of the breed. This means that both stud dog and bitch should be evaluated by a qualified breeder to determine if they have the correct conformation and temperament for breeding. Both animals should be tested for inherited diseases prior to breeding (see the list of inherited problems below).

When you are satisfied that the dog is of breeding quality, the search can begin for a suitable mate. The proper breeding partner will have had the same tests as your dog, and the two lines will be compatible. This means that you or the breeder must know the lines of the animals in question as far back as the great-grandparents.

Some Acquired and Inherited Health Problems of Boston Terriers

The following list of medical problems associated with the Boston terrier should be considered prior to purchasing a dog of this breed. If your Boston terrier has any of these conditions, or if any existed among its ancestry line, talk to your veterinarian before breeding your dog. Find out if the condition is inherited, whether it will pose a threat to the life of bitch or her puppies, and what treatments are available.

Cataracts: This is an opacity of the lens of the eye that causes poor vision and blindness. There are two types: juvenile and recessive. Cataracts can appear in young dogs as well as older animals.

Mastocytoma: This is a skin tumor. It starts as a thickening of the skin, especially on the hind legs, and develops into a nodule that should be removed.

Hemivertebra: An abnormal development of the vertebrae which can result in neonatal death or to chord compression, which can lead to paralysis. Generally, this will occur in the tail, ribs, or throat area.

Luxating Patella: This is a malformation of the femur that causes lameness at about four to six months of age.

Craniomandibular osteopathy: A growth in the mouth which causes discomfort when eating. Malnutrition can result, as well as intermittent fever to 104°. This condition usually starts at around four to seven months and may last until the dog is thirteen months, when it can be expected to regress and resolve.

Aortic and Carotid Body Tumors: These are tumors of the main artery for the heart as well as the artery which supplies blood to the brain.

Distichiasis: In this condition two rows of eyelashes develop, usually on the upper lid, causing irritation.

Anasarca: Multiple heart defects or dysplasia of the lymphatic system. The result is that the puppies are born with oversize bodies, because of which they have been nicknamed *Walrus* or *rubber* puppies.

Swimmers: An inability to stand at four to six weeks of age. Causes a flattened chest.

Hydrocephalus: Fluid on the brain.

Deafness.

Esophageal Achalasia: Laxity of the esophagus muscle.

Walleye: Blue and white iris.

Cushing's syndrome: Caused by an adrenal or pituitary dysfunction resulting in obesity and muscular weakness.

Cleft Lip or Palate: A split in the lip or roof of the mouth.

Patent Ductus Ateriosus: The heart valve does not close.

Endothelial Dystrophy: The cornea degenerates.

Cross Eye.

Hernias.

Getting Ready To Breed

Once you have found a suitable mate for your dog, there are steps you can take which will make the breeding safer, and which will result in healthier puppies.

First, before the breeding takes place, you can worm the bitch. This must be done under the

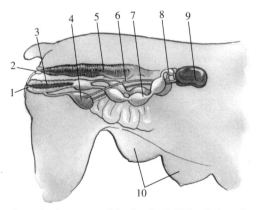

Reproductive organs of the female: 1. Vulva 2. Anus 3. Vagina 4. Bladder 5. Rectum 6. Ureter 7. Developing embryo 8. Ovaries 9. Kidneys 10. Teats

supervision of your veterinarian. By worming her just before she is bred you will reduce the possibility of passing worms from dam to puppies before they are born.

Just before being bred, both bitch and stud should be checked by a veterinarian to determine that they do not have infections such as brucellosis, a bacterial disease that can destroy your dog's breeding future, harm the puppies, or even abort a litter, or any other illnesses or inherited problems such as those listed above.

Within two to three weeks after being bred, the bitch should be put on a special dog food designed for pregnancy.

The Estrus Cycle

A female Boston terrier will come into season (or heat) about every six months. The first can occur between six and nine months of age. However, a bitch should not be bred until she is two years old, to insure that she is fully mature, and to give you time to have her genetically tested. By two years she will also have had time to earn an obedience title and maybe some points toward her championship.

Normally, the heat cycle will follow four stages. During the first, the ovaries will start to produce eggs. As the eggs mature the uterus will thicken. A bloody vaginal discharge will occur that can last from four days to two weeks. During this time the vulva will swell.

In the next stage, the discharge will become less bloody and can turn clear, with a mucous consistency. It is during this phase that mating should occur.

Ovulation, the third stage, usually takes place between the ninth and fourteenth day of the cycle (counted from the first sign of bloody discharge). This stage can last as long as nine days and the bitch remains fertile during the entire period.

Breeding Your Boston Terrier

If the bitch has been bred, the next six to eight weeks constitute the *metestrus* phase. The puppies begin to form, and the dam's body prepares to nurse them. If she has not been bred she will return to an *anestrus* stage, in which her ovaries and uterus revert to an inactive state.

The Stud Dog

If, after thinking very carefully about breeding and the responsibilities it means for the next fifteen or so years (the lifetime of a puppy), you still want to produce a litter of Boston terriers, you must find a good stud dog. If you have contacted all of the breeders you can find, and studied a number of dogs, you should have some idea which male, and which lines, are going to produce what you want in a Boston terrier.

The male you choose must be the best quality available, and an excellent specimen of the breed. Ideally, you will want one who has earned an obedience title, or has shown his intelligence and temperament in some way, as well as championship conformation. Neither your bitch or the male should have obvious flaws that can be transmitted genetically.

Like the female, the male should be at least two years old. If you have never bred your female before, make sure the male is experienced. It will make the breeding easier, both for you and your dog.

Generally, you will take your bitch to the stud's home, since males usually breed better in their own territory.

Be sure that the terms of the breeding are written up in the form of a contract. You will want the stud fee (payment to the owner of the male) in writing. If the fee is to be paid in puppies, that should be clearly stated, as well as related matters, such as who chooses the puppies who will serve as fee, what will happen if there are no puppies born, or only one, etc. Boston terriers do not have large litters.

You will want your lawyer to review the contract. So many people find out too late that the wording of a contract has made them the loser when things do not go as planned.

You will want to be present when the actual breeding takes place. This will insure that the male you chose will be mated with your bitch. And, if she does not become pregnant, you should be allowed a second breeding at no charge.

Most breeders will want to see the bitch before the breeding. If this is not possible, they will want to see photos and study her pedigree. If the breeder has not seen your dog before, there is a chance that she may be refused. This would only occur if your bitch is not the quality you thought. But if you've done your homework and arranged everything in advance, there should be no problem.

You must keep in mind that the owner of the male will want to produce the best puppies possible. The reputation of the stud dog rests on what he produces, and the owner will not want to take a chance on breeding to a dog who could produce inferior or low-quality puppies. If a stud dog produces too many poor-quality puppies, the demand for his stud services will decline, and the breeder

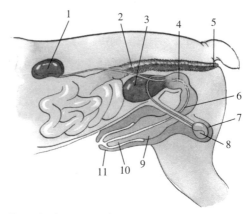

Reproductive organs of the male: 1. Kidneys 2. Rectum 3. Bladder 4. Prostate 5. Anus 6. Urethra 7. Scrotum 8. Testes 9. Bulb 10. Penis 11. Sheath

will gain an unfavorable reputation in the dog world. The stud owner's goal (and it should be yours as well) is to produce the next Top Champion Boston terrier.

The Breeding

Before the actual breeding takes place, you should have devoted considerable time to preparation for the event. Your bitch will have been recently examined by your veterinarian and declared to be in the best of health. She will have been wormed and will be up to date with all of her shots and genetic tests. Her good condition is essential to a successful mating, pregnancy, and delivery. Keep in mind that the best sire in the world cannot overcome poor health or bad genes in the dam.

Try to breed your bitch on the ninth day of her heat cycle. Many breeders like to do a second breeding on the eleventh day, to insure that the breeding takes. If she is to be shipped, you must allow adequate time for her to rest prior to the breeding.

When the dogs actually breed, you may have to muzzle the bitch. This is an especially good idea for her first mating, because she may try to bite the male. One person should be available to hold the male, and another the female. After they connect they will **tie** (copulate) for about fifteen minutes. It helps to allow the dogs to stand on a nonslip surface, such as a rug.

Once your bitch has been bred it is important to keep her away from all other males. She can be bred again during her cycle and have a litter which is actually sired by two different males. One of those may not be a Boston terrier, which will mean that some or all of the puppies will be mixed breeds.

Sometimes the breeding does not take, yet the bitch will show the signs of pregnancy. This is called **false pregnancy.** This is a serious medical condition, and surgery (usually removal of the uterus and ovaries) may be required to correct the problem.

If your dog conceives, she will have her puppies around the 63rd day after breeding. If you've bred her on both the ninth and eleventh day, you will not be sure which day will be number 63.

When a Boston terrier is carrying only one or two puppies it may be difficult to be certain that she is pregnant. You should take her to your veterinarian for check-ups from the sixth week on to determine if she is pregnant and whether or not there is a problem.

During this time do not allow your dog to play roughly, or to engage in a great deal of exercise. Brisk walks are fine until such time as it becomes uncomfortable for your dog. Be sure to consult with your veterinarian. Be sure to handle her with care, especially when picking her up. Generally, it is not a good idea to carry your bitch around during the last few weeks of pregnancy.

Whelping a Litter

Because almost three-quarters of all Boston terrier bitches must have caesarean sections, it is important to stay in touch with your veterinarian. It is a good idea to have your veterinarian examine the bitch during the last week or so of pregnancy, to determine that the puppies are alive, and to assess the possibility of complications.

Long before your bitch is due, you should have the *whelping box* ready. This is an enclosed area, large enough to accommodate the bitch and her puppies. She should have room to move around, and also to lie down at a distance from her puppies if she wants to get away. It should be about the size of a child's playpen and, in actuality, some playpens will make good whelping boxes.

You can make a whelping box, purchase one, or adapt one from something else. It can be as simple as a sturdy carton with the sides cut down, or specially constructed of wood or plastic. Place it in a quiet area of the house, away from traffic, and should be set up a few inches off the floor to avoid dampness, drafts, heat, and dirt.

It is important to keep both bitch and puppies warm. If the spot where you put the whelping box is on the cool side, you can provide a special heating pad for the new family. You can purchase such a canine heating pad at your local pet-supply store, or through mail-order companies. (Do not use a regular heating pad. It can become too hot and burn the puppies.)

Be sure to line the whelping box with newspaper, using only the black and white printed parts and not the colored sections. (If possible, obtain unused newsprint from a moving company.) You can also use old towels folded or laid out so that they are flat. Be prepared to change the lining of the whelping box numerous times a day, especially as the puppies get older.

Introduce the bitch to the whelping area about two weeks before the due date. Quite likely, your bitch will not appreciate your efforts on her behalf, and will prefer to give birth in another spot. You may have to train her to go to the whelping box, or even keep her confined there until after the puppies are born.

The pressure of the unborn puppies on her bowels and bladder will make her have to relieve herself more frequently, so be sure to take her out often.

Before she whelps, clip your dog's nails short and file them smooth, to avoid scratching the puppies.

Labor

Within a day or so of the due date, your dog may become uncomfortable and restless. She may tear up her whelping bed and try to rearrange everything. By providing old, clean towels or a blanket, you will give the bitch something to do

The whelping box can be made of almost any material as it is sturdy, warm, and dry. It should prevent the puppies from getting out, yet allow the bitch the freedom of coming and going as she wishes.

and keep herself busy. If she seems short of breath, it is because the puppies are being carried high, crowding the heart and lungs. Call your veterinarian if she seems very distressed or has too much difficulty breathing.

Take your dog's temperature daily from day 58 until delivery. Use a rectal thermometer and plenty of vaseline. Her normal temperature should be about 101.2°. A drop to about 98° is usually a sign that she should whelp within the next 8 to 24 hours. At this time she may appear to have chills. She will drink and urinate a great deal. She may also appear constipated, but do not try to give her a laxative or help her in any way.

As your dog gets close to whelping, she may pant heavily or even vomit. You may see a discharge from the vagina. Be sure to let your veterinarian know that your bitch is ready to whelp.

When her temperature goes up to 100° you can expect her to whelp within an hour or two. If delivery does not begin within that time, and if she seems to be having difficulty, you should call your veterinarian, because she may need a C-section.

When she starts whelping, you should alert your veterinarian that the birth is in process. Just because she whelps the first puppy with no difficulty does not mean that the rest will go as smoothly. Here are some danger signs:

- Difficult labor for more than 45 minutes without delivering a puppy
- Passing dark-green or bloody fluid before the birth of the first puppy
- A puppy gets stuck in the birth canal and does not come out, but rather moves back and forth with each contraction
- Labor stops

If any of these situations develop, you should take your dog to the veterinarian immediately.

After your bitch whelps a puppy she will pull away the sac that covers the puppy and chew through the umbilical cord. If she does not do this last, you will have to do it for her with a pair of sterile scissors, being very careful to tie off the chord. (Be sure to discuss this with your veterinarian in advance.)

Hopefully the bitch will clean the puppy and get it to nurse. If she does not do this you will have to wipe the puppies yourself. Use a soft towel and be sure that each one is breathing.

If the bitch does not nurse the puppies, you will have to contact your veterinarian and find out how to bottle-feed them. You must use a special formula as a milk replacement—you cannot use cow's milk.

It is important for the veterinarian to examine the bitch after she delivers all of the puppies so that you can be sure she has passed all of the after-birth. You should also have all the new puppies examined to determine that they are healthy and do not have heart or lung defects.

The Puppies

The first four days after birth are the most critical for the puppies' health. Possible causes of death during this period include the following:
- The mother did not receive a proper diet during pregnancy.

- The mother did not have proper or up-to-date vaccinations.
- A puppy got chilled.
- A puppy suffered birth trauma.
- A puppy was physically immature.
- A puppy had a lethal congenital defect.
- A puppy developed an infection.

If the puppies survive the first four days, they have a good chance of growing up to be healthy puppies.

You should call your veterinarian if you notice any of the following:

1. After the first 24 hours the puppy should start to gain weight. If it does not, call your veterinarian.
2. The puppy has not stretched its legs or straightened its body out by the third day.
3. The puppy shows signs of deafness by two weeks.
4. The puppy's eyes have not started to open by two weeks of age.
5. From birth to three weeks of age the puppy cries for more then 15 minutes before falling asleep.
6. The puppy seems cold, limp, and does not want to nurse, or does not try to crawl back to its mother and littermates when taken away from them.
7. The puppy seems to have difficulty breathing.

After the First Week

Beginning when the puppies are 24 hours old, you need to check and record their weight every

A judge checks a contestant's conformation (top). An eager Boston terrier demonstrates his skill at scent discrimination during an advanced obedience trial (bottom).

week. You should also keep a record of each puppy's appetite, stool quality, and temperature. If you are going to have any cosmetic surgery performed you should make arrangements with your veterinarian as soon as the litter is born. Dewclaws, for example, should be removed by the time the puppies are three days old. The eyes should be checked for entropion before the puppies reach two and a half weeks of age. Entropion, which may lead to blindness, is a rolling inward of the upper and/or lower lids, causing the lashes to rub against the eyeball.

When the litter is a week old you should register it with the American Kennel Club. You will receive a form for each puppy. By the time the puppies are ready to be placed in their new homes, you should have the forms in hand.

Socializing the Puppies

The socialization process starts as soon as the puppies are born. While they may not seem to be aware of you during the first few days, they can sense that you are there. Once or twice each day you should gently talk to the puppies and handle them. You can pick them up and softly stroke their little bodies while you talk to them. These sessions should only last for about two minutes.

By the time the puppies are about four weeks old you can handle them a bit more. Be sure to hold them in your hands on their backs for a few seconds. This will get them used to being in this position.

As these handsome portraits clearly reveal, the Boston terrier packs a great deal of dog into a small package.

When they reach five to six weeks, you should take each puppy away from the litter for a brief period and allow it to interact alone with you. There should be no roughhousing, but rather a nice, calm interaction with a toy. This will let the puppy get used to being away from the litter and learn to trust humans.

After the puppies have their first shots you can allow friends and neighbors to visit and gently play with them for short periods of time. The goal is to teach the puppies to enjoy the company of people. By the time they are ready to go to their new homes they should be well adjusted and trusting animals.

Selling the Puppies

You can start to take orders from prospective buyers when the puppies are around five weeks old, but they should not be sold until seven to eight weeks. If you plan to ship a puppy by air, many airlines as well as state regulations require that the puppy be eight weeks of age. Be sure to call the airlines to check their requirements.

When weaning puppies, make sure that each one gets enough food and is not crowded away from the dish. (Even giving each pup a dish will not solve the problem as the pups will steal from each other.)

Breeding Your Boston Terrier

You should give yourself plenty of time to interview each prospective owner. Ideally, this should be done in person, but it can also be done long distance. You can ask the new owners to videotape their home and neighborhood, so you can see where the puppy will live. You will want to determine if they are going to give your precious Boston terrier puppies a good, loving home. Ask questions such as:

1. Why do you want a Boston terrier?
2. Where do you plan to keep your new puppy?
3. Have you owned dogs before? If so, what happened to them?
4. Do you own pets now?
5. Are there children in the family, and, if so, what are their ages?
6. How much time do you have to devote to the training of the puppy?
7. Who is your veterinarian?
8. Who is your dog trainer?
9. Have you consulted with either or both about this puppy?
10. Do you have a puppy-proofed fenced yard?
11. Do you plan to spay or neuter your puppy?
12. Do you plan to show this animal at any point?

It is your job as a quality breeder to determine if the people who want your puppies are capable of taking proper care of them. You must also try to find out which puppy has the temperament that will most closely fit the lifestyle of your customer.

You should give a guarantee against major inherited health problems for any puppy you sell. A three-year guarantee is the minimum, and a lifetime guarantee is preferable. And you must be willing and able to provide support, in the form of advice and information, for your customers if they should have any problems at any time in the future.

If you have special requirements for prospective buyers, they should be put in writing in the form of a contract, read and signed by everyone involved. Be sure to spell out all of the details, including the "if—then" clauses (see page 59 above). The contract should clearly state what you guarantee and what are the responsibilities of both you and the new owner. Legal advice will be beneficial.

When the puppy is ready to be sold you should provide the following for the new owner:

1. The name and address of your veterinarian.
2. All certificates and records of shots and veterinary care.
3. The AKC registration form.
4. Information about the puppy's diet—how much, what, and when to feed it.

As a quality breeder with excellent puppies to sell, you can expect, for the most part, to have pleasant relationships with your customers. There is nothing quite so rewarding as receiving a special note from a happy family with a snapshot of your puppy, now a happy, healthy adult. This will be possible with the investment of enough effort, time, and money to breed quality dogs.

You can feel a special pride when one of your puppies earns an obedience title or a championship, and even more so if one becomes *a therapy dog*, making hundreds of people happy throughout the dog's lifetime.

Training Your Boston Terrier

Getting Started

There are almost as many methods of dog training as there are dog trainers. However, you must keep in mind that training is actually a process of *teaching* the dog what *you* want it to do.

The training is carried out by means of repetitive exercises. The dog is taught to perform certain actions in response to specific cues given by you. The cues come in three categories:
1. what you say (the *Command*),
2. how you say it
3. the movements you make.

Remember that dogs do not speak English, therefore, *how* you say it will mean more than *what* you say, and what you *do* will be more important still.

It is also important to follow a few simple rules when training a dog.
1. Be consistent in your actions as well as your commands. You cannot call a dog to come to you by using the word "Come" one time and "Here" the next. When you call your dog, you cannot let it walk to your side one time and sit in front of you the next, and so forth.
2. Give a command once. Do not tell your dog to sit, for example, three or four times. If you do this you are actually teaching the dog that (a) it does not have to listen to you right away, and/or (b) it does not have to listen to you at all.
3. Be fair. You should not punish your dog. Suppose someone put an advanced calculus problem on a piece of paper, told you "This is a math problem. Do it!" and then slapped you when you did not solve it immediately. How would you feel? This is exactly what some training methods do to a dog.

Most dogs are very eager and willing to please us if they understand what we want. Therefore, it is important to show exactly what you expect your dog to do.

4. Praise or correct immediately. Dogs associate praise or correction with what they are doing *at that moment.* If your pet chews on something, then walks over to you and you give correction, it will assume that you are correcting it for coming to you. You cannot explain that you are actually angry with the dog for chewing.
5. Only ask your dog to work as long as it is able. The younger the dog, the shorter the training session. The longest session for any dog should be about 10 minutes. Also, give serious consideration to the weather conditions at the time of training. Boston terriers cannot tolerate hot, humid weather. It would be unreasonable to ask your dog to work for you if the weather is uncomfortable.

The most important part of training is praise for a job well done.

6. Only ask your dog to do as much as it can understand. Again, the younger the dog, the smaller the request. If you have not taught your dog to understand you, it will become confused. Training is teaching.
7. Set up your training sessions so that the dog can win. Your pet will gladly respond to you if it is praised for doing the exercise correctly. You should always praise and reward your dog, even if it means that you have to set things up so that it wins.
8. Only train your dog before its main meal, or two to three hours or more after the main meal. Few people (and dogs) want to go out and exercise right after they eat a big dinner. You will find your pet much more responsive if you let it digest its food first, or if you have your session before the meal.
9. Make sure that everyone who comes in contact with your dog uses *your* commands. It is very difficult for a dog to understand what you, or anyone else, expects it to do if you use different words for the same command. An example of this would be if different people used the commands "Lay down," "Down," "Rest," or "Get" when the dog is supposed to lie down.
10. Be sure to match your tone of voice with the command. You should try to sound enthusiastic and upbeat. Your dog will be more willing to interact with a bright, happy person than a grouch. If you are always harsh with your dog, it may come to fear you. It is much more enjoyable to have a dog who enjoys working *with* you.
11. Think like a dog. Of course, no one knows for sure just how a dog thinks, though scientists have developed some very interesting theories. One thing, however, seems clear. What is important and meaningful to humans is not necessarily important and meaningful to dogs. For example, dogs can see much better at night than humans, there-

fore they never need a light outside in the dark. No matter how many times a dog watches humans turn on a light switch, it will not learn to do this on its own, because it sees no benefit to itself in having the light on. (When dogs are trained to assist the handicapped, they are taught to turn on light switches on command. But they will not do it on their own.)

If you want your dog to learn something, make it meaningful to your dog. There are two main interactions between you and your dog that make anything meaningful to it. One is praise from you and the other is food. By associating either or both with an activity, it will become meaningful to your dog.

12. Do not punish your dog. Encourage the behaviors you want, rather than punishing those you do not want. Many people fall into the trap of correcting their dogs for not following their commands, rather than praising when their pet performs properly. Your dog expects praise for doing something good. It will not assume that your silence *also* means that it performed correctly. You must praise what is correct for the dog to understand which behavior is the one you want.
13. Each dog has a favorite activity or object. It may be a game or a toy. Most dogs have a number of foods they dearly love. All of these positive things can be used as rewards for the behavior you want to encourage.
14. Corporal punishment should never be used. Use of such punishments as leash jerks, hitting, electronic shock, or other unpleasant things can cause your dog to become afraid of you.
15. Negative reinforcement is not the same as punishment. It is an instant and consistent unpleasant result to a given undesirable activity. Negative reinforcement is something the dog can stop simply by stopping undesirable behavior. An example is the choke chain. As

the dog pulls, the choke chain chokes the dog. As soon as the dog stops pulling, the choke chain stops choking the dog. The problem with choke chains is that they can injure a Boston terrier, and many times the dog would rather put up with the choking action of the collar to get at what it wants, and will continue to pull.

16. Always give "Start exercise" and "End exercise" commands. Many people do not use these commands. They assume that the dog will understand when the lesson is to begin or to end, but this is not the case.

It is especially important to give an End-exercise signal. This command should be used only when the training session is over, not after each step.

Here is an example of what can happen if you do not use an End-exercise command. You tell your dog to "Sit-stay," and walk away, forgetting about the dog. Theoretically the dog should sit forever, but it will not. At some point the dog will break the Sit-stay. What happens then is that the dog learns that you really do not mean what you say, or that it can break the command when it feels like doing so. When you give your dog choices, it will often make choices you cannot accept.

When you choose a release command, try to pick a word which is not commonly used. "Okay" is fine if you do not use it a great deal in your everyday language. "Finished," "Done," and "End" are all words you can use. The word itself is not important because dogs do not speak English. What is crucial is that you use the same word each time.

17. Do not play during training sessions. This is important because the dog must not confuse the casual interaction you have together during play and the serious relationship that you should have during work.

18. Keep a record of your progress. It is not unusual for a dog to reach a plateau where it seems that no gains are made. You can become discouraged at these times and forget how much you have actually accomplished. If you keep a record of how you and your dog do, you will realize during the frustrating times that you have actually made quite a bit of progress.

Equipment

You will need a few pieces of equipment in order to train your dog.

- A six-foot leash, made of nylon webbing, leather, or canvas. You should not use a rope or chain leash.
- A collar that goes around the dog's neck. For very young puppies either a buckle-type collar or a modified choke collar can be used. The modified choke collar is one which is soft and does not choke the dog completely, such as the Premier collar made by Premier Pet Products. The Premier collar can also be used for adult dogs. The neck collar is the one that stays on the dog at all times.
- Another very good training device is a head harness. This appliance can be very useful if used properly. With a small modification, most head harnesses can be used on a Boston terrier. You can purchase a head harness at your local pet supply store.
- Treats. These should be of a consistency that can be handled easily, as well as cut up into very small, 1/4-inch pieces. Use treats as a teaser, which the dog will work harder to get more of, not as a meal that your dog has to sit and eat. Treats are used as a reward, not as a bribe.

Basic Commands

Here follows a list of the basic commands you should teach your dog, along with exercises with which to teach them.

Training Your Boston Terrier

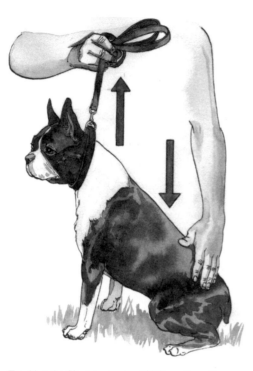

Teaching the Sit. As you say, "Sit," gently pull up on the leash while you push down on the rump.

Sit: The purpose of this exercise is to teach your pet to sit on command. Place the dog on your left side. Gently take up the slack in the leash while you guide the dog's hindquarters down to the ground, simultaneously telling it to Sit. If you use a head harness, gently tilt the dog's head back, guide the hindquarters down, and give the verbal command to Sit.

As soon as the dog's hindquarters rest on the ground, praise it verbally and give it a pat on the head. Do not allow the dog to wiggle around while in the sit position. If it does this, gently reposition it, and give praise as soon as it becomes quiet.

Do not ask your dog to sit for very long, especially at the beginning of training. Sometimes, especially in the early sessions, you may only have a few seconds to give praise. A ten-second sit is a fair length of time for starters. Be sure to watch closely and praise immediately when your dog gives you a nice, quiet sit.

As soon as you accomplish your goal, give the dog permission to get up. As your pet begins to get the idea, you can ask it to sit for longer periods of time—up to one minute—and to sit in the exact position you wish.

Walk with Me or Walk: Either of these is the command you give your dog when you want to go for a casual walk in the park. The dog is allowed to have the full leash, and to walk anywhere it wants to within the range of the leash. This means it can walk in front of you, behind you, can stop, or do whatever it wants, as long as it does not break the rules of the exercise. The rules are simple: The dog cannot lead, and it cannot pull.

To begin, give the command and start to walk. If your dog pulls, very gently change direction as you call the dog's attention to the fact that you are doing so. This is how it works. As you are walking, your dog starts to forge ahead of you and pull. Abruptly, without hesitation, change direction while saying "Hup! Hup! Hup! Walk." You cannot stop and wait for your dog, because it will then learn that if it pulls, you will stop while it strains to sniff an interesting smell.

As soon as it starts to walk in your direction without pulling, praise your dog as if it has performed a miracle.

After a few days of this you will be amazed at how your dog will pay attention to you and watch where you go. If you use a head harness you will find that the dog will give in sooner and walk much better. This is because every time you change direction, the dog's head will follow you. As soon as this happens you can praise the dog for paying attention to you.

Training Your Boston Terrier

It is very important not to jerk the dog with a head harness or any other kind of collar. You can do serious injury to its neck and spine. This is especially true with puppies.

Heel: The purpose of this exercise is to teach your dog to walk quietly by your side without pulling. While "Walk with me" is used for casual walking, "Heel" is the at-attention-and-behave command. It is usually used when you are in a crowded area and you want to be sure that your dog is safely by your side. It is also used for obedience trials.

Proper Heel position is when your dog sits quietly by your left side, the dog's right shoulder even with your left leg. To do this, position your dog in that manner and tell it to "Sit." With the dog in Heel position, first get its attention by calling its name, and, about one second later, give the command "Heel" as you start walking with your left leg. Encourage your dog to walk with you by sounding upbeat or slapping your leg.

When it starts to walk with you, praise your dog with a pat on the head and a hearty "Good dog." After heeling for about a minute, stop and give a "Sit" command.

As your Boston terrier learns what you want, it will sit automatically when you stop. If it is reluctant to Heel with you do not drag it along, but rather encourage the dog to follow you. Be sure to praise your dog each time it Heels the way you want, even if only for a few seconds. Dog training is accomplished moment by moment!

Stay. To teach your Boston terrier to Stay, you must be sure that the dog knows how to Sit. Place the animal at your left side in heel position. Firmly hold the dog in place by the leash, simultaneously giving a firm "Stay" command. Immediately leave the dog, starting off with your right foot. At the same time bring the palm of your left hand down in front of the dog's face. Step away from the dog, turning as soon as you are in front of the dog so as to face it.

Keep eye contact and watch for any attempt to get up. If the dog does attempt to get up, gently tell it to Sit and Stay again. If it does get up, simply reposition your dog and start over. If you use a head harness you can keep the dog's head from going down, which discourages it from getting up.

Only ask the dog to Stay for about ten seconds, at which time return to its side in Heel position. To properly return to the dog, walk toward it, keeping your left side closest, and then continue around behind it until you are again in Heel position. Gradually, as the dog learns to Stay, you can

Teaching the Heal. Train your Boston terrier to walk on your left side. Be sure to use a happy tone of voice.

71

Teaching the Stay. With your palm toward your dog, give a firm Stay command.

walk to the end of the six-foot leash and increase the staying time to one minute. Once you have accomplished this, you have taught your dog the Sit-stay.

Recall. Once the dog has mastered the Stay command you can teach it to Come when called. Put the dog in a Sit-stay position and leave, going

Teaching the Recall. With an upbeat "Come," call your dog to you. Be sure to praise your pet when it obeys.

to the end of the six-foot leash. After waiting one minute, give the dog a very happy-sounding "Come." You can clap your hands or open your arms wide, inviting your dog to rush to you.

As soon as it reaches you, give a Sit-stay command, making sure that your pet stops right in front of you. As soon as it does, give the dog a lot of praise.

There is one thing you must never do. If your dog does something which displeases you, and then comes to you, never, *never* scold or otherwise show anger toward it. The dog will not understand that you are angry at it for something it did 20 minutes ago "over there." The only thing your dog will learn is never to come to you when you call. It takes a long time to regain a dog's trust once you lose it.

As your dog learns to Come on command, you can use a longer leash to make it Come from further away. You should also practice this exercise in as many different places as you can, so the dog can learn to come to you no matter where you are.

Down. To teach your dog to lie down on command, you should first put it in a Sit-stay position. It will be easier to teach this command if one end of your dog is down already.

Stand next to your pet in the Heel position. With the dog in a solid Sit-stay, gently run your right hand down the front of its face, so that its eyes will follow your hand to the ground. As you do this, gently pull down on the leash. If you are using a head harness, pull down and a little out so that the dog's head is guided to a spot about 6 inches (15 cm) in front of its feet, to give the dog a feeling of going down.

In some cases the animal will not get the idea to follow your hand into a Down position. If this happens, you can use a treat to lure it into a Down position. If you use one, you must be careful not to hold the treat so far in front of the dog that the dog wants to get up to go after it.

If you choose not to use a treat you can gently pull the dog's front legs out, so that it goes into a

Training Your Boston Terrier

Teaching the Down. If necessary, you can gently lower your dog to the ground by extending its fore paws forward.

Down position. Press down on the dog's shoulders as you pull the dog's legs forward, gently guiding it to a Down position. Make sure that you do not unbalance your dog.

You should constantly encourage your dog to go down, and praise it if any attempt is made to move toward the ground.

Once it is in a Down position, tell it to Stay. After a few seconds give a Sit command, followed by a Release. At this point you can praise your dog some more.

As your dog gets the idea and learns to lie down on command, you can increase the time the dog stays down up to three minutes. Be sure to return to your dog after each Down exercise and give the Release command.

Go To Heel. This exercise is used to finish off the Recall exercise. First, you must put your dog in a Sit-stay position. Next, call it to you using the Recall command. When the dog is sitting quietly in front of you, give the "Go to heel" command. At the same time, take a small step backward, just to get your dog moving, and lead it to your right side, around the back of your body, and into the

Heel position on your left. The dog should finish this exercise in Heel position by your left side.

All of your obedience exercises should be practiced every day until the dog listens to you in a reliable manner. Since it will be expected to listen and obey no matter where you are, you should practice your obedience exercises in different places. Practice in town, in the country, in the park, in your home, in your backyard, at playgrounds, at shopping malls, etc. Always remember when training your dog outside to check the weather. You should not practice outside in the heat of a summer day, nor should you make your dog walk on surfaces, such as blacktop, which are too hot. Remember that Boston terriers have difficulty in the heat.

Obedience Classes

It is a very good idea to take your Boston terrier to obedience class, or your puppy to puppy kindergarten. There are a number of options available.

You can enroll your dog in a class offered by a local dog trainer, or by a dog-training club.

Every Boston terrier should receive obedience training. Classes give you and your dog a chance to socialize.

These usually consist of about 10 to 20 other dogs and owners, and typically meet once a week. You will actually teach the dog yourself under the guidance of the trainer.

Another possibility is to have private sessions with a trainer, who will tailor the sessions to your dog's abilities. You will be responsible for daily practice sessions. Some kennels offer the option of boarding your dog while having it trained for you. If you decide this is the way to go, be sure to check the facility and its reputation carefully. Since you will not be there, you will never be certain of the treatment your dog receives. (This is the least desirable way to train your pet. Participating yourself allows an opportunity to form a special bond with your Boston terrier. It can also be great fun for the two of you.)

Beyond Basic Obedience Classes

There are many activities for you and your Boston terrier to enjoy. Some are highly organized, while others are quite casual.

You can compete in obedience trials at dog shows. There are a number of obedience titles your dog can earn, such as Companion Dog (CD), Companion Dog Excellent (CDX), Utility Dog (UD), Tracking Dog (TD), Tracking Dog Excellent (TDX), Obedience Title Champion (OTCH), and Canine Good Citizen certificate (CGC).

You can also earn a Therapy Dog certification for your Boston terrier, which certifies you to take it to nursing homes for the residents to pat and play with, or to facilities which house other disadvantaged people, such as the mentally handicapped.

Other working dog titles you can try for are Versatile Canine Companion and Versatile Canine Companion Excellent, which are earned through an accumulation of working titles.

You can get involved in *agility,* which is a sport where you and your dog run a special agility course. *Flyball* is another activity that Bostons can enjoy. In this game the dog is taught to press a lever that releases a ball, and then catch it.

If your dog is good enough, you can enter it in conformation shows, which judge physical beauty according to breed standards.

No matter what activities you undertake with your Boston terrier, it will always be a loving pet and companion who will give you years of joy and fun.

The Problem Dog

Unfortunately, even with the best of training and care, a dog can develop undesirable behaviors. There are many factors which can help to produce misbehavior, the most important of which are the dog's temperament and the inadvertent training of undesirable routines.

A dog's temperament, which is formed out of its inherited mental health plus reactions to its

Correct bad habits promptly, firmly, and consistently.

upbringing, can cause it to react negatively in certain situations.

It is also possible to teach your dog unfortunate habits, often without even noticing that you are doing so. Many times people will do things with their dogs to satisfy their own needs and communicate an altogether different message to the dog. Established undesirable behaviors can usually be corrected with a little patience and know-how.

Aggression Toward Owners

Although this is not a common problem with Boston terriers, it does happen on occasion. Aggression toward owners should not be mistaken for a puppy's play and mouthing. It usually occurs in older dogs, although younger animals can display aggression as well. A growl toward an owner should be considered aggression, especially if it seems intended to precede a bite.

The owner can bear some of the responsibility for producing an aggressive dog. Some of the reasons that trigger aggression are scolding, punishment, and overprotectiveness toward objects and food.

If your dog bites you in a hostile manner it is normal for your feelings to be hurt. You may feel as though your dog has betrayed you. In many cases, people who have been threatened or bitten by their dog will not have the same level of confidence when working with it in the future, and can even become afraid of their pet.

The first step in dealing with a dog who has shown aggressive behavior is to *stop all physical punishment*. Most dogs bite because they feel threatened. If you physically attack your dog you will make it feel more defensive. Remember that you appear overwhelmingly gigantic and powerful to your Boston terrier.

You should not use time out as a punishment either. Many people think that if they put their dog outside, it will sit alone and feel bad, but this is not so. Putting the dog outside may actually be a reward if the dog likes to be outside.

The best way to deal with an aggressive dog is to isolate it socially. Have no interactions with the dog at all, other than for feeding, watering, walking, and giving directions. Avoid all petting and praise, except during training sessions, which should occur at least once a day. Stop all treats, but make sure you feed your dog twice a day.

You should continue the social isolation until you notice a change in the dog. Instead of demanding what it wants, the dog will start to crave your approval and attention. Of course, you should consult a qualified canine behaviorist to help you with this problem.

Carsickness

Carsickness can be caused by stress. When a puppy is taken from its litter for the first time, it is usually taken into a car right away. That's a big negative association. Lack of early socialization and handling can also make a puppy insecure in a car. If you have a small Boston terrier puppy, be sure to turn it on its back a few times a day.

Carsickness often results when a bossy dog feels as though it is out of control of its environment. To cure this, you must make the dog accept you as its leader. To make this happen, you will need to make the dog earn all its praise and attention by doing something first.

Let's say your dog likes to be picked up or petted. First make the dog sit or lie down, and then give it a quick pat, or just pick it up long enough to say "Good dog." Then put it down immediately. Associate praise and reward with performance.

Next, you want to get your dog to associate fun with the car. Start by letting the dog get into the car when it is parked. Give the command to get into the car, and as soon as your dog does, praise it and let it have a favorite toy. Then immediately let the dog get out of the car. Repeat this process over several days, until you see your dog eagerly jump into the car when you give the command.

Next, over several more days, lengthen the time the dog spends in the car. Finally, take short trips, gradually lengthening them. At the end of the process your pet should be able to ride in the car without stress.

Chewing

All dogs chew, and there is no point in trying to stop them. The best you can do is to teach them which items can be chewed and which can't.

Chewing in puppies is second nature and a part of growing up. Young puppies chew to explore their environment and to learn. Because they do not have hands as we do, dogs use their mouths to manipulate and hold things. It is our job to teach them which things are off limits for them.

There are some preventive steps you can take with your puppy to avoid a chewing problem. First, never give it old clothing of any kind to play with. How do you expect it to understand or to tell the difference between its old clothing and your new clothing? Never give your puppy leather toys or chews either. Again, the puppy can mistake your good leather products for the toys. Do not give it sticks to play with. Not only are they unsafe, but you will encourage your puppy to chew everything in your house made of wood.

Chewing is a way to relieve stress. Avoid excited departures when you plan to leave home for a period of time, and try to ignore your puppy (until it settles down) upon your return. This will only increase your pet's stress when you leave. If your dog does chew something while you are away, do not pay attention to the mess when you come home. Clean it up when the dog does not see you doing it.

If your pet persists in chewing certain objects around your house, you can give those objects an unpleasant taste by spraying them with one of the many anti-chew products on the market, such as "Bitter Apple." You can also use some of the stronger mouthwashes, such as Listerine.

Persistent chewers must be given the social isolation treatment as described above. This will lessen their loneliness when you leave and thus decrease their stress.

Fearfulness

Dogs can be fearful of many things in life, and one of the saddest things to see is a little Boston terrier who is abnormally timid. Often, an owner's frightened response to some event will cause the dog to become even more fearful. If your dog reacts to the pop of a firecracker, for instance, it may recover from the noise without incident. But if you, or another human, gets upset and calls attention to the event, you may actually be teaching the dog to get upset as well.

The best thing you can do when a dog is fearful is to ignore the situation. Do not try to comfort it. The dog will misunderstand your actions as praise for behaving in a fearful manner.

The first thing you must establish is that you are the dog's leader. This will allow it to follow your example. You should make your pet earn all affection and petting. Do not spoil your dog by petting it excessively, nor should you treat it in an unusually harsh manner.

Once you see that your dog is responding positively to you, you are ready to recreate the frightening situation. Set the stage to reenact the fearful event, using whatever props are appropriate, and be sure to have your pet's favorite toy on hand as well. Then bring your dog into the picture.

As you start enacting, start a play game with the dog. The goal is to get the dog to associate a happy activity with the fearful one. Soon the dog will look forward to the situation as an opportunity to play, rather than as something to be afraid of. You can do this exercise a few times a day, but

Paper training. Leaving a scented bottom layer will help your puppy find the right place to relieve itself.

not too close together. If the dog is very fearful or if you do not feel confident working with the problem consult a canine behaviorist.

Submissive Urination

When a dog or puppy wets as it is approached by a human or animal, it does not realize it is urinating. Therefore, you should not scold your pet for doing this. Correction will only make the problem worse and more difficult to cure. Submissive urination is part of very early puppy behavior, and is normal from birth until weaning. The mother dog initiates the behavior as part of the cleaning process for the puppies.

Usually, as the puppy grows up the submissive urination stops. If it does not, here are a few tips you can use to cure the problem.

First, take careful note as to when this occurs. Is it when you talk to the dog, come home, scold it, lean over it, etc.? Make sure that during such times you do not approach or act toward the dog in a threatening manner, but rather act very friendly and welcoming.

Sometimes you will need to avoid eye contact with the dog, or crouch down and let it come to you. You may also have to avoid talking to your dog as you approach it. Be sure to enlist the help of other people with this cure so that the dog is not submissive to all people.

If changing your attitude toward the dog does the trick, be sure to give the dog time to gain confidence.

Jumping on People

Often puppies will rise up onto their hind legs, wanting to be picked up. It is one of their ways of letting you know they want attention. As a dog gets older this reaching up can become jumping up. Even though the reason, craving for attention, is the same, what seemed cute in a puppy is often unacceptable in an adult. Mature dogs who exhibit this behavior have been rewarded for it since puppyhood by being petted and receiving attention.

If you are wearing old clothes, and if you are a dog lover, you may not mind your dog jumping up. But if you have on good clothes you will not be happy. Guests in your house will almost always mind it if a dog jumps on them, even if it is a cute Boston terrier. And although Bostons are not large enough to knock an adult over, they can cause a child or an elderly person to stumble and fall.

If you truly enjoy having your dog jump on you, then you should teach the dog to do this on command only. This way, the dog can be invited to jump when you desire it, rather then whenever it gets the urge.

There are two kinds of jumping. The type described above is friendly jumping and is the kind of good-natured physical contact the dog desires with humans. The second type of jumping is more assertive and pushy. Usually you can recognize this by the dog's attitude, and also by the fact that if you do not stay still the dog will become more physical and may become upset, jumping with more determination. The assertive jumper is usually aggressive in other areas of interaction as well.

The best way to cure a jumping dog is to teach it to do something else when it feels the urge. To do this, you must first teach the dog to obey the Sit-stay and Come commands. If you see the dog coming in your direction and you have enough time, give the dog a firm Come command. A dog that has been trained in the Come command should approach and sit in front of you. Super praise from you is in order. If your dog does not do this, give it a firm "Sit-stay" command, and gently guide it into position. Praise the dog when it relaxes into a sitting position in front of you.

If you do this every time the dog tries to jump, it should only take a few weeks for it to learn to sit instead of jumping. Be sure to instruct your friends and guests not to allow your dog to jump. Well-meaning dog lovers can undo in minutes what it took you and your dog weeks to achieve.

The Overprotective Dog

A dog can become overprotective toward almost anything, including you.

Sometimes you may have brought on overprotectiveness in your pet through the messages you have sent it. For example, if you feel threatened and fearful, especially of strangers, you may have praised the dog for showing protective behavior. Since your pet cannot make the same types of judgements as you, its protective behavior can rapidly develop into a problem situation in which it will go after any stranger who comes to your home. Sometimes a dog will become overprotective because of the owner's general insecurity in his or her relationship with the dog. In both cases the way to deal with it is the same.

First, you must assume a leadership role. The dog must *earn* all praise and attention from you. Next, you should to start a socialization program, similar to that for puppies (see page 65). You

must show your dog how to behave by acting friendly toward people.

Sometimes it will help if you have people give a small treat to your dog when it goes up to them. You can also bring along a special ball or toy that strangers can use to play with it. Generally, you will want the dog to learn that strangers are not to be feared.

Many people will wonder if the dog will protect them in the event of an intruder in the home. Socializing a dog will not lessen its protective abilities at all. On the contrary, the dog who knows which situations are acceptable and which are not will be a better protector. The dog will be much happier without all of the worry associated with its need to protect you from everyone who comes along.

If your dog's overprotectiveness has progressed to the point where it has actually bitten someone, you have a problem on your hands. Consultation with a canine behaviorist is definitely indicated.

Barking

Sometimes a dog will bark excessively. This can occur both in the house and outside. A typical response to a barking dog is to yell at it to be quiet. But unless you teach your dog what the command "Quiet" means, the dog may think that you are just barking too. After all, if you take away the meaning of the English word "Quiet" as it is generally yelled at a barking dog, what does it sound like?

Before getting into the cure for barking, you should first consider why the dog is barking. Is it because the dog is alone, bored, frustrated, being teased? If any of these is the cause of the barking, your best bet would be to remove the cause. Often this will be enough to solve the problem.

If your dog barks at appropriate times but just a little too much for your taste, you can train it to bark only within the limitations you set. First, teach your dog to speak on command. To do this, tease your dog with food and give a "Bark" command until it gives a frustrated bark. Immediately reward the dog with the food.

Once you have your dog barking on command, you can give it the command "Bark," followed by the command "Quiet." As you say "Quiet," extend your hand with a treat. Your dog cannot bark and sniff at the same time. As soon as it stops barking, praise your dog and give it the treat. Your dog will soon learn to stop barking when you say "Quiet."

Rooting In The Trash

This can be a frustrating problem. The dog gets to eat what it finds in the garbage, so the trash acts as its own reward. If you catch and scold your dog it may learn to stay out of the trash when you are around, but may jump back in the minute your back is turned.

To cure a dog from going in the trash, you must make the trash punish the dog. Although mousetraps are a popular remedy for this problem, they can hurt and even cause damage. A better way is to blow up a balloon and put it on the top of the trash. As the dog goes into the trash, the balloon will pop and the dog will find that the trash is not as nice as it thought. After a few tries the dog will give up making forays into your garbage.

Housetraining Your Boston Terrier

Small dogs can be more difficult to housetrain for a number of reasons. First, if a small dog urinates on your carpet you may never realize it because the spot is so small. However, the scent will remain and invite the dog to go there again. Second, to the small dog your house can seem very large and the far corner very distant. The cor-

ner, therefore, may seem far enough away to be considered out of the living area, and appropriate to use as a toilet area. Therefore, it is important that you do not allow your Boston terrier to have a free, unsupervised run of your house until you are certain that it is housetrained.

There are certain times when your puppy will need to go out. Generally these will be upon waking up, shortly after eating, and after a play session, but you really should watch the puppy carefully at all times.

If you see your puppy sniffing around, looking for a "spot," take it outdoors immediately. That way, it will learn to associate elimination with being outside, rather than in the house.

The key element in housetraining is to set up the situation so that the dog understands what is expected. You should designate a specific place outside, which can be as small as five feet square. This spot will become the dog's potty area. When you take your pet out for a nature break, go directly to that area. You may have to carry very young puppies to the spot, as they may not be able to control themselves long enough to reach it.

When you have the dog at its potty spot, allow it to go. As soon as it starts, say a word that will become your pet's potty command. Use this word each time the dog goes. When it is finished you should make a big, happy fuss, patting, praising, and even giving your dog a treat.

As you continue to practice this exercise, the dog will start to give you a signal indicating that a trip to the toilet area is necessary. But sometimes your pet will give you the same signal just to go out for a romp. To tell which is which, you can ask if it is a potty trip, using your special word. If so, the dog will get very excited and let you know. If not, you will get a look as if to say "Are you kidding?"

If you stick to this program your dog will learn to go in the area you've designated. The exercise will work with dogs of any age, but the older the dog, the longer it will take to train.

Training Your Boston Terrier

Introducing New Babies and Pets

From time to time a new member is added to the family. This could be a baby, an older person, a cat, a dog, or some other pet. And sometimes your Boston terrier may not welcome this addition. This could be especially true if the new arrival is a mature dog.

If an adult dog is coming into the household, the best way to handle the situation is to make arrangements for the two dogs to meet on neutral ground. Neither dog will feel as though the other is an intruder into its territory, and they will be more likely to become friends. After a few visits you can walk both dogs to your home. This way you avoid putting either dog in the situation where one is an intruder and one a defender of the home.

If the new addition is a baby, you must pay close attention to the amount and quality of time you spend with your dog before the baby's arrival. Afterwards, try to keep the amount and quality of time with the dog unchanged. Do not get angry at the dog for its curiosity toward the baby. Nor should you correct your pet in such a way that the dog could associate the correction with the baby. You should make contact with the baby a happy playtime for the dog, even though you are the one who will be playing with the dog and not the baby. This way the dog will associate the baby with the fun times it has with you.

Contact between baby and dog is a very personal matter. You will have to set the limits. Always consult your pediatrician regarding this, and do what you feel is best. If at any time you do not feel comfortable allowing your dog to be around the baby, do not permit it.

When a baby starts to crawl or walk, your dog may react with renewed interest. Always try to make the encounter a happy time for the dog by playing with it. Never scold the dog for going near the baby, never leave the baby and dog together unsupervised.

As soon as your baby starts to move around you should start to teach the child how to behave toward animals. Never leave an unsupervised toddler around your dog. No matter how friendly they are toward each other, a Boston terrier can be hurt by a falling child. The child will want to pull ears, poke eyes, and otherwise explore the dog as if it were a toy. This should not be allowed.

With a little planning and thought, children and dogs can get along just fine. They can grow together, forming a special bond that adults often seem to miss.

Some Cute Tricks To Teach Your Boston Terrier

There is nothing quite as delightful as seeing a dog perform tricks. The dogs love the attention and enjoy pleasing you. If your pet learns some tricks, you can entertain children, or even the elderly and shut-ins at a nursing home. A dog who performs simple tricks can bring a great deal of joy into many people's lives.

Before you start to teach your dog tricks be sure that it is physically able to perform them. Each dog is different, and some may have difficulty where others may not. This is the most enjoyable form of dog training, and both you and your dog should have fun.

Always use a release word as discussed in the previous chapter (see page 69) to let your dog know that the training session is over. And have a ready supply of treats on hand. Remember, treats should be a tease and not a meal. The ideal size is a pellet 1/4-inch square.

Your dog should already be competent at all the basic commands. Of course, the very first step is to get the dog to pay attention to you when you speak to it. "Come" is a good exercise for this. By teaching your dog to come when you call, you will reinforce it for paying attention to you. The next important command is "Sit-stay." You must be able to hold your dog's attention as well. See the chapter on dog training for this exercise.

Go To A Particular Spot: This is the basis for many of the tricks you will want your pet to learn. Set up a small platform for it to sit on. The platform must be low enough so that your dog can easily get up on it. It must also be stable, and not move around under the dog. A small foot bench with a rug stapled to it will work well for the Boston terrier.

With your dog on a leash and sitting in front of you, point to the bench and give the command as you point to the bench. The command can be any word you choose to use, such as "Up." Simultaneously, gently lead your dog to the platform and place it up on it. As soon as your pet is up, praise it and give it a treat. Practice until your dog will go onto the platform on command.

Shake Hands: Give your dog a "Sit-stay" command. Reach down, grab a paw, and hold it out as if you are shaking it. At the same time, give the command "Shake hands." Do not pump the paw up and down until the dog knows the trick. As you are holding the dog's paw, reward it with verbal praise and a treat.

Saying Prayers: You will need your platform or a small stool, just high enough to allow your dog, when seated, to rest its front paws on the platform. Sit your pet in front of the platform. As you give the command "Say Your Prayers," place the dog's paws on the stool while the dog remains in a sitting position. Immediately hold a small piece of treat between your dog's paws in such a way that your dog must place its nose between its paws to get the treat. Keep the dog in that position for a few seconds and than say "Amen" and allow your dog to get up.

By practicing this exercise your dog will learn to walk over to the stool, place its paws on the top of the stool and hold its nose over its paws until you say "Amen."

Sit Up: To teach your dog to sit up, you can either use a stick or the corner of a wall for support. Place your dog in a Sit-stay position. Next, help it sit up by raising both of its front paws. As the dog holds this position, give it a treat and praise.

Balancing Food: Put your dog in a Sit-stay position. Gently but firmly hold its nose in the palm of your hand. With your other hand, place a small piece of food on the tip of your dog's nose. Hold its nose so that it cannot get the food, and give the command "Wait." Then give a release command and let go of its nose.

Generally the dog will learn, after a number of tries, to flip the food into the air and catch it.

Take a Bow: While your dog is standing, place one of your arms around its belly in a hugging position. Your other hand is placed on top of its head. Gently lower the front half of the dog toward the ground, with the front legs extended and the head lowered, simultaneously giving the command "Take a bow." Hold the dog in this position for a second as you reward it. Then give a release command and lots of praise.

Play Dead: Put your dog in a Sit-stay position and then into a Down-stay. Next, as you give the command "Play dead," gently push the dog over onto its side and hold it in that position for a few seconds. Then give the release command, followed by praise. As the dog gets the idea, increase the amount of time you make it stay in the Play-dead position, so that the dog learns not to get up until told to do so.

Crawl: Find an object that is just tall enough for your pet to crawl under, such as a footstool. Place the dog on one side of the object and give a Sit-stay command. Then go to the other side of the object. Give the Down command, then call your dog and encourage it to come to you by crawling under the object. When it starts to do the right thing, give the command "Crawl." Repeat this until your dog learns to go down and crawl toward you on command. Gradually raise the height of the object until your pet will crawl on the floor without needing an object to crawl under.

Useful Literature and Addresses

Addresses

American Kennel Club, 51 Madison Ave., New York, NY 10010.

Boston Terrier Club of America
Contact the American Kennel Club for the current address (which changes every two years).

International Veterinary Acupuncture Society, Meredith L. Snyder, VMD, 2140 Conestoga Road, Chester Springs, PA 19425. You may write to Dr. Snyder for a list of licensed veterinary acupuncturists.

United States Department of Agriculture (301-436-7833)

Books and Articles

American Kennel Club, *The Complete Dog Book.* New York: Howell, 1985.

Baer, Ted. *Communicating With Your Dog.* Hauppauge, NY: Barron's Educational Series, Inc., 1989.

_____. *How to Teach Your Old Dog New Tricks.* Hauppauge, NY: Barron's Educational Series, Inc., 1991.

Benning, Lee Edwards. *The Pet Profiteers.* New York: Quadrangle/The New York Times Book Co., 1976.

Bulanda, Susan. *The Canine Source Book.* Doral, 2619 Industrial St. NW, Portland, OR 97210.

Campbell, William E. *Behavior Problems in Dogs.* Goleta, CA: American Veterinary Publications, Inc., 1992.

Dangerfield, Stanley & Howell, Elsworth. *International Encyclopedia of Dogs.* New York: Howell Book House, 1974.

Frye, Fredric. *First Aid For Your Dog.* Hauppauge, NY: Barron's Educational Series, Inc., 1987.

Jones, Arthur F. & Hamilton, F. *The World Encyclopedia of Dogs.* NY: Galahad Books, 1971.

Mill, Charles E. Jr. *How Safe Is Air Travel for Dogs,* American Kennel Gazette, Dec. 19, 1992, p. 71.

Pinney, Chris C. *Guide to Home Pet Grooming.* Hauppauge, NY: Barron's Educational Series, Inc., 1990.

Ullmann, Hans. *The New Dog Handbook.* Hauppauge, NY: Barron's Educational Series, Inc., 1984.

Ward, Amy, DVM. *Small Animal Health Care: A Primer for Veterinary Clients.* Edwardsville, KS: Veterinary Medicine Publishing Co., 1983.

Weitzman, Nan & Ross, Becker. *The Dog Food Book,* Charleston, SC: Good Dog!

Index

Index

Index

Index

Perfect for Pet Owners!

"Clear, concise...written in simple, nontechnical language."

AFRICAN GRAY PARROTS Wolter (3773-1)
AMAZON PARROTS Lantermann (4035-X)
BANTAMS Fritzsche (3687-5)
BEAGLES Vriends-Parent (3829-0)
BEEKEEPING Melzer (4089-9)
BOSTON TERRIERS Bulanda (1696-3)
BOXERS Kraupa-Tuskany (4036-8)
CANARIES Frisch (2614-4)
CATS Fritzsche (2421-4)
CHINCHILLAS Röder-Thiede (1471-5)
CHOW-CHOWS Atkinson (3952-1)
COCKATIELS Wolter (2889-9)
COCKATOOS Lantermann & Lantermann (4159-3)
COCKER SPANIELS Sucher (1478-2)
COLLIES Sundstrom & Sundstrom (1875-3)
CONURES Vriends (4880-6)
DACHSHUNDS Fiedelmeier (1843-5)
DALMATIANS Ditto (4605-6)
DISCUS FISH Giovanette (4669-2)
DOBERMAN PINSCHERS Gudas (2999-2)
DOGS Wegler (4822-9)
DOVES Vriends (1855-9)
DWARF RABBITS Wegler (1352-2)
ENGLISH SPRINGER SPANIELS Ditto (1778-1)
FEEDING AND SHELTERING BACKYARD BIRDS
  Vriends (4252-2)
FEEDING AND SHELTERING EUROPEAN BIRDS
  von Frisch (2858-9)
FERRETS Morton (2976-3)
GERBILS Gudas (3725-1)
GERMAN SHEPHERDS Antesberger (2982-8)
GOLDEN RETRIEVERS Sucher (3793-6)
GOLDFISH Ostrow (2975-5)
GREAT DANES Stahlkuppe (1418-9)
GUINEA PIGS Bielfeld (2629-2)
GUPPIES, MOLLIES, PLATYS
  Hieronimus (1497-9)
HAMSTERS Fritzsche (2422-2)
IRISH SETTERS Stahlkuppe (4663-3)
KEESHONDEN Stahlkuppe (1560-6)
LABRADOR RETRIEVERS Kern (3792-8)

LHASA APSOS Wehrman (3950-5)
LIZARDS IN THE TERRARIUM Jes (3925-4)
LONGHAIRED CATS Müller (2803-1)
LONG-TAILED PARAKEETS Wolter (1351-4)
LORIES AND LORIKEETS Vriends (1567-3)
LOVEBIRDS Vriends (3726-X)
MACAWS Sweeney (4768-0)
MICE Bielfeld (2921-6)
MINIATURE PIGS Storer (1356-5)
MUTTS Frye (4126-7)
MYNAHS von Frisch (3688-3)
NONVENOMOUS SNAKES Trutnau (5632-9)
PARAKEETS Wolter (2423-0)
PARROTS Wolter (4823-7)
PERSIAN CATS Müller (4405-3)
PIGEONS Vriends (4044-9)
POMERANIANS Stahlkuppe (4670-6)
PONIES Kraupa-Tuskany (2856-2)
POODLES Ullmann & Ullmann (2812-0)
PUGS Maggitti (1824-9)
RABBITS Fritzsche (2615-2)
RATS Himsel (4535-1)
SCHNAUZERS Frye (3949-1)
SCOTTISH FOLD CATS Maggitti (4999-3)
SHAR-PEI Ditto (4834-2)
SHEEP Müller (4091-0)
SHETLAND SHEEPDOGS Sucher (4264-6)
SIAMESE CATS Collier (4764-8)
SIBERIAN HUSKIES Kenn (4265-4)
SMALL DOGS Kriechbaumer (1951-2)
SNAKES Griehl (2813-9)
SPANIELS Ullmann & Ullmann (2424-9)
TROPICAL FISH Stadelmann (4700-1)
TURTLES Wilke (4702-8)
WATER PLANTS IN THE AQUARIUM Scheurmann
  (3926-2)
WEST HIGHLAND WHITE TERRIERS
  Bolle-Kleinbub (1950-4)
YORKSHIRE TERRIERS Kriechbaumer & Grünn
  (4406-1)
ZEBRA FINCHES Martin (3497-X)

Paperback, 6 ½ x 7 ⅞ with over 50 illustrations (20-plus color photos)   Barron's ISBN prefix: 0-8120

Barron's Educational Series, Inc. • 250 Wireless Blvd., Hauppauge, NY 11788
Call toll-free: 1-800-645-3476 • In Canada: Georgetown Book Warehouse
34 Armstrong Ave., Georgetown, Ont. L7G 4R9 • Call toll-free: 1-800-247-7160

Order these titles from your favorite book or pet store.